Reassessing Activism and Engagement Among Arab Youth

To the memory of Malek Sghiri.

PEACE, CONFLICT AND VIOLENCE SERIES: 3

Reassessing Activism and Engagement Among Arab Youth

Edited by Sarah Anne Rennick

First Published in 2022 by Transnational Press London in the United Kingdom, 13 Stamford Place, Sale, M33 3BT, UK.
www.tplondon.com

Transnational Press London® and the logo and its affiliated brands are registered trademarks.

Requests for permission to reproduce material from this work should be sent to: sales@tplondon.com

Paperback
ISBN: 978-1-80135-117-1
Digital
ISBN: 978-1-80135-118-8

Cover Design: Nihal Yazgan
Cover Photo by Uta Scholl on unplash.com

Transnational Press London Ltd. is a company registered in England and Wales No. 8771684.

REASSESSING ACTIVISM AND ENGAGEMENT AMONG ARAB YOUTH

Edited by

Sarah Anne Rennick

TRANSNATIONAL PRESS LONDON

2022

CONTENTS

ABOUT THE AUTHORS

Layla Baamara is a political scientist specialising in commitment, collective action, and protest mobilisations. Since 2009, her research has relied on fieldwork conducted mainly in Algeria and has focused on political parties, neighbourhood committees, young members of associations, and electoral campaigns. She recently co-edited the book *Cheminements révolutionnaires. Un an de mobilisations en Algérie* (2019-2020), published by CNRS editions. Researcher at the Institut de recherche sur le Maghreb contemporain in Tunis, her new research programme is about student movements and engagements.

Asef Bayat is Professor of Sociology, and Catherine & Bruce Bastian Professor of Global and Transnational Studies at the University of Illinois, Urbana-Champaign. Before joining Illinois, he taught at the American University in Cairo for many years; and served as the director of the International Institute for the Study of Islam in the Modern World (ISIM) holding the Chair of Society and Culture of the Modern Middle East at Leiden University, The Netherlands. His research areas range from social movements and social change, to religion and public life, urban space and politics, and contemporary Middle East. His recent books include *Being Young and Muslim: Cultural Politics in the Global South and North* (ed. with Linda Herrera) (Oxford University Press, 2010); *Post-Islamism: The Changing Faces of Political Islam* (Oxford University Press, 2013); *Life as Politics: How Ordinary People Change the Middle East* (Stanford University Press, 2013. 2nd edition), *Revolution without Revolutionaries: Making Sense of the Arab Spring* (Stanford University Press, 2017), *Global Middle East: Into the 21st Century* (ed. With Linda Herrera) (University of California Press, 2021), and *Revolutionary Life: The Everyday of the Arab Spring* (Harvard University Press, 2021).

Hadia Kawikji is a Syrian certified attorney at law since 2004. She is the co-founder and a Non-Resident Senior Fellow at the Omran Center for Strategic Studies, founded in 2013. She has more than 14 years' experience in governmental a non-governmental organizations in human rights, political affairs, and mediation in the Syrian peace process. She also has several publications in English and Arabic, and has participated as a speaker in dozens of events at the international level. In early 2016 she joined the High Negotiation Committee that is representing the opposition delegation in the Syria talks in Geneva as a consultant. During the Syrian crisis, she trained a number of local councils and local communities in Syria on governance, mediation skills, gender issues, and conflict analysis. She has a Master of Advanced Studies in Mediation in Peace Process from ETH Zurich, Switzerland (2019), and an International Master in Legal, Social, and Economic Sciences from Foggia, Italy (2007).

Khaled Nasser, PhD, is a family communication consultant who specializes in trauma management, parenting, and couples therapy. Nasser practices at his private clinic in Beirut, where he also administers neurofeedback training. He also provides trauma therapy and training sessions to refugee communities and journalists exposed to tensions in the Middle East. Nasser is a lecturer in Communication at the Lebanese American University (LAU) and the American University of Beirut (AUB). His research currently focuses on mapping the trauma impact among Arab journalists covering tensions in the Middle East.

Sarah Anne Rennick (editor) is the deputy director of the Arab Reform Initiative, an adjunct lecturer in Political Science at Sciences Po Paris, and a guest researcher in 2022 at the Centre for Advanced Middle East Studies at Lund University. Her research focuses on social movements, mobilization, and alternative forms of political engagement in the Arab region. More particularly, her work explores patterns and spaces of youth mobilization and civic and political participation, and various factors influencing when and how youth engage in collective action. She also works on Arab diaspora mobilization in the post-2011 period, exploring transnational/translocal political remittances and their impact on the creation of new identities, solidarities, and political practices in both host and home sites. Her book *Politics and Revolution in Egypt: Rise and Fall of the Youth Activists* (Routledge, 2018) involves a culturalist analysis of the revolutionary youth social movement that became a dominant social force during the 2011 Egyptian uprising. She holds a dual PhD in political science from Lund University and the Ecole des Hautes Etudes en Sciences Sociales.

Mounir Saidani is Professor of Sociology at the High Institute of Human Sciences, Tunis Al Manar University, Tunisia. He is interested in socio-anthropology of culture, knowledge and art, and socio-cultural change in contemporary Tunisia and the Arab World. He has published several books and articles in Arabic, French, and English in Tunisia and abroad. He has also translated books and articles in the field of his interest from French and English into Arabic. One of his latest publications is a 1,418 page report on the Religious State in Tunisia 2011-2015, a collective work on which he served as general supervisor and the editor in chief. He is leading a multidisciplinary research unit working on "Knowledges, Cultures, and Social Change" and is a member of the Executive Committee of the International Sociological Association. He has given lectures and presentations in A Coruña, Ajman, Ankara, Beirut, Brussels, Doha, Gottingen, Liège, Manama, Oran, Paris, Rabat, Santiago di Compostela, Taipei, Toronto, and Tunis. He is the Editor in Chief of the Tunisian Review of Social Sciences, edited since 1964 by the Centre for Economic and Social Studies and Research (CERES, 1962). He also coordinates the XVII ISA PhD Students Lab (September, 2022).

ACKNOWLEDGEMENT

Chapters 1-4 were carried out with the aid of a grant from the International Development Research Centre, Ottawa, Canada.

No financial interest or benefit has arisen from the direct applications of this research.

INTRODUCTION

Sarah Anne Rennick

Among the many outcomes of the Arab uprisings of 2011 was the collective recognition that we had not been paying enough attention to our conceptual understanding of youth or the variety of forms that political activism can take in a region that seemed to have grown morose under its authoritarian yoke. The vibrancy of the social movements that manifested in public spaces across the region in 2011 demonstrated the limitations of analytical frameworks such as 'waithood,' 'bulge,' and 'apathy' for understanding the region's youth and their relationship to politics. These gaps in knowledge drove forth numerous studies and multilateral research projects that have added significant conceptual depth to the notion of 'youth' that move well beyond age-based cohort definitions, as well as critical insight into the indirect or seemingly 'non-political' forms of Arab youth political activism. Such works have allowed us to conceive of youth within the frames of Mannheimian generational analysis, and have allowed us to see political participation outside of formal instances such as elections and parties. Yet at the same time, there remain conceptual gaps with regards to the analysis of 'youth politics' as well as the various factors that mediate a distinctly youth political behavior.

The collection of works presented in this volume seeks to contribute to this body of literature by delving into the concept of 'youth politics' and making explicit how various forms of civic engagement in seemingly 'apolitical' fields can indeed be conceived as a form of political activism by utilizing an alternative analytical framework for understanding 'youth' and their relationship to the political. Carried out from 2016-2019, the empirical research presented here draws on evidence gathered through semi-structured interviews, focus group discussions, and policy dialogues with over 100 youth activists in Algeria, Tunisia, Lebanon, and Syria representing sectors ranging from arts promotion and urban beautification to work with children and community development. The research design began from a shared puzzle regarding how youth themselves understand and qualify their various forms of engagement, seeking to enter the

1   lifeworld of youth activists to understand their collective schemata for
2   interpretation of what constitutes 'politics' and 'the political'. In
3   speaking with youth who actively participated in their country's
4   uprisings in 2011 (in the case of Tunisia and Syria) or who almost ten
5   years later were on the streets demanding radical change to the system
6   (in Algeria and Lebanon), what is striking is their own insistence on the
7   continuity between these forms of direct political protest and their civic
8   engagement. Yet at the same time, these activists almost universally
9   qualify their civic engagement as expressly 'apolitical' and indeed do
10   not necessarily identify a political content to their civic activism. Such
11   reflections beg two questions: how do youth understand the notion of
12   'apolitical' engagement, and on what premise do they see continuity
13   between political protest and so-called 'apolitical' civic engagement?

14   To answer these questions, the four chapters in this volume utilize
15   the analytical tools of practice theory in order to assess Arab youth civic
16   engagement as a form of political activism. Here, 'youth' is understood
17   as a generational practice of politics, meaning a 'competent
18   performance' of shared knowledge and understandings of politics and
19   the political, as well as a collective identification of the sources and
20   vectors of change, that informs their various forms of engagement and
21   participation. In conceiving of youth in these terms, this unorthodox
22   collection – which represents multidisciplinary and multilinguistic
23   research and which specifically includes both the theoretical and
24   practitioner perspectives – is able to bring to the fore how youth
25   comprehend and indeed dichotomize their own forms of engagement
26   with 'politics' and the political. Finally, in a conceptual reflection in the
27   conclusion, this volume advances a framework for understanding what
28   constitutes a 'youth politics' and provides analytical leverage for
29   assessing how youth political behavior – as in the Arab uprisings in
30   2011 and again in 2019 – can act as transformative agent.

Youth as a Generational Practice of Politics

32   While the 2011 uprisings shined a global spotlight on Arab youth as
33   the political avant-garde, important research into their various patterns
34   of political participation pre-dates the Arab Spring by at least a decade.
35   In the years preceding 2011, a number of studies emerged, ranging
36   from individual ethnographic accounts of emerging youth activist
37   groups (see for example Onodera 2009 and Hassabo 2009) to broad

1　comparative studies captured in books and edited volumes (such as
2　Lust-Okar and Zerhouni 2008) and numerous journal articles that
3　contributed to our understanding of the patterns, spaces, and
4　modalities of youth political engagement. These works debunked the
5　notion of a depoliticized or apathetic youth cohort by problematizing
6　the effect of exclusion in formal political processes and institutions and
7　the resulting process of self-isolation from formal political
8　participation. Such research found, for example, that Arab youth are
9　indeed quite interested in politics and hold firm political opinions, but
10　that they prefer to express these in alternative domains and spaces,
11　such as blogs and socially-networked virtual groups (see for example
12　Radsch 2008). Likewise, this work pointed to the need to rethink the
13　spaces where youth political participation takes place and indeed what
14　can constitute political activism. In his seminal work, Bayat (2010), for
15　example, placed emphasis on youth 'nonmovements' and the
16　accommodation strategies of youth that nonetheless represented a
17　form of political claim-making on existing power structures. Likewise,
18　Shehata (2008) explored the diverse channels and means of political
19　engagement and the move away from university campuses towards
20　other forms of protest and associational work. This research also began
21　the work of pinpointing not only where Arab youth political activism
22　was taking place, but indeed how it was occurring. Beyond the online
23　sector, for example, this work was demonstrating the preference for
24　non-institutionalized formats away from the traditional NGO, the
25　preference for youth-led and horizontal decision-making structures,
26　and the dominance of political protest as the preferred mode of
27　activism.

28　　In the years following the 2011 uprisings, this research on Arab
29　youth political activism increased markedly. A number of multilateral
30　research projects, such as Power2Youth and the SAHWA Project, both
31　funded by the European Union, emerged to investigate the cohort of
32　youth in order to assess issues related to exclusion, participation,
33　values, and prospects in political, social, and economic terms with the
34　aim to promote policy options for inclusion. Using a mix of
35　quantitative and qualitative methods and comparative work facilitated
36　by the consortium nature of such projects, these research programs
37　looked in particular at the forms and sectors of youth political
38　participation in the aftermath of 2011 and largely confirmed a
39　continuation of the patterns and modes established in the preceding

1   years. Such work thus documented the types of non-formalized
2   political institutions created by youth activists in the immediate
3   transition periods (Korany and El-Sayyed 2017), the non-
4   institutionalized spaces where youth pronounced their political views
5   (Zerhouni 2017), and the preference for protests and informal
6   associations or social movements in the form of political activism (Sika
7   2017). Elsewhere, Abdou and Skalli (2018) confirmed the fluid
8   boundaries and blurred lines between the civic and the political, and
9   how seemingly apolitical engagement in CSOs prior to 2011 translated
10   to direct political protest a few years later, whereas Amara (2012)
11   demonstrated how non-political spheres could be infused with political
12   activism. In this vein, Onodera, Lefort, Maiche, and Laine (2020)
13   explore how life trajectories and latent political engagement embedded
14   within personal aspirations can collapse the rigid boundary between
15   'politicization' and 'depoliticization'.

16   Added to this work, though, was a distinct effort to rethink not only
17   what Arab youth political activism consists of, but indeed to rethink
18   the notion of 'Arab youth' itself. Indeed, a distinct research agenda
19   emerged that sought to reconceptualize what is meant by 'youth'. Much
20   of this work focused on the concept of political generation, as
21   developed by Mannheim (1923) and his conceptual descendants, and
22   the associated development of specific political consciousness.
23   Hassabo, for example, explored how shared lived experience formed
24   the basis of generational consciousness, and how this in turn drove the
25   desire for an expressly 'youth' venue for contestation. Similarly,
26   Onodera argued that youth activists shared formative experiences of
27   protest and political uprising that fueled collective political identity.
28   Bayat, on the other hand, argued that youth as social category should
29   be understood as shared habitus, behavior, and cognitions that are
30   socially constructed in the period between childhood and adulthood.
31   Finally, Murphy (2012) put forth a conceptualization of youth as a
32   shared generational narrative of exclusion, marginalization, and
33   alienation in order to assess the Arab Spring and the political
34   preferences and behaviors of youth expressed therein. These various
35   conceptualizations of youth and their utilization of generation theory
36   have focused largely on the role of lived experience in the formation
37   of shared cognitions, political consciousness, and the push towards
38   explicitly youth-led forms of collective action.

1   The empirical chapters presented here seek to contribute to this
2   literature in two ways. First, while much of the literature has attempted
3   to look at different forms of civic and seemingly non-political
4   engagement in the pre-2011 period as alternative forms of political
5   engagement that were a precursor to the Arab uprisings, we move the
6   other direction, specifically problematizing Arab youth civic
7   engagement in the post-2011 period as alternative forms of political
8   activism and indeed an alternative manifestation of the claims made
9   during direct protests. In particular, we focus on civic engagement that
10   is not only taking place in seemingly non-political sectors but those
11   actions that are expressly called 'apolitical' or 'not related to politics' by
12   the activists themselves and assessing how these seek many of the same
13   goals of 2011, albeit by other means than direct contestation or direct
14   claim-making on the State. Second, we render explicit how an analytical
15   concept of 'youth' can be used to further understand youth political
16   activism in the Arab region, and in particular the blurred lines between
17   the political and the seemingly apolitical as well as the distinctive modes
18   of Arab youth political activism, and how these reflect generationally-
19   located ideas regarding politics and change.

20   As our starting point, the works presented here propose a new
21   conceptual framework for understanding 'youth' in analytical terms,
22   focusing on how their own understanding of what the term means and
23   how it informs their activism. The youth activists researched here very
24   purposely place emphasis on their quality of 'youth': they adamantly
25   revindicate their youthfulness and its relationship to particular patterns,
26   modes of action, and narratives. Given this, the research presented here
27   operationalizes the term 'youth' as an analytical tool that can be used
28   to assess a set of practices that are generationally determined and locally
29   specific. Drawing on practice theory, we put forth the concept of
30   'youth' as a form of political practice, located in both direct political
31   protest but also in 'apolitical' civic engagement. This political practice
32   is underscored by collective understandings of politics/the political and
33   shared views about the sources and vectors of change. This practice is
34   also imbued with distinct consciousness of specific generational
35   location and generationally determined narratives regarding the State
36   and its pillars.

37   As an analytical framework for examining social life, practice theory
38   encompasses certain views regarding human agency and social action,

1 placing at the fore knowledge and interpretation and how they become
2 collectively manifested in actions, thought processes, and joint
3 enterprises. Practice theory places its analytical emphasis on practices,
4 a conceptual term referring to the tripartite combination of routinized
5 bodily action, cognitive processes, and socially embedded
6 knowledge/understanding. Practices can be understood as 'competent
7 performances' (Adler and Pouliot 2011): they are socially meaningful
8 patterns of action and thought that express shared knowledge and
9 understandings. They include bodily forms of action, such as skill-
10 based routines or 'ways of doing' but also discursive and cognitive
11 activity, such as collective interpretations or 'making sense'. Practices
12 are by their nature collective, iterative, and repetitive, produced by
13 interactions between individuals. As such, they reflect subjective and
14 intersubjective meaning.

15   Importantly, practices also reflect organizational context: practices
16 are linked to social categories or particular organized settings, and thus
17 act as distinctive markers of collectivities. To this point, the studies
18 presented here have sought to think of activist groups specifically as
19 'communities of practice', (Wenger 1998), or organized clusters of
20 likeminded individuals who are characterized by specific practices that
21 represent the collective understandings and interpretations that the
22 community has regarding itself and its action. Communities of practice
23 share a sense of joint enterprise and create repertoires of action,
24 interpretation, and linguistic codes that sustain their particular
25 practices. Participation in a community of practice involves a process
26 of social learning as well as identity formation that can nonetheless
27 transform according to changes in membership and in a dialectic
28 relationship with the broader social and political environment.

29   Background knowledge and understanding – interpretations,
30 assumptive schemes, intentions, ascribed meanings, both implicit and
31 explicit, – play a key role in the formation of practices. Each specific
32 practice is informed by specific knowledge and understanding derived
33 from historical-social context and a shared view of social reality held
34 by a given collectivity or organizational setting. Practice theory
35 emphasizes historical-social location and the simultaneous
36 reproduction and contestation of order, norms, and meanings through
37 practices. Practice theory thus proves a powerful theoretical framework
38 for exploring differences in understanding and interpretation that are

1 linked to specific social and organizational settings and how these
2 impact patterns of action.

3   In conceiving of 'youth' as a generational practice of politics, and
4 thinking of activist groups as communities of practice, the studies here
5 have delved into the youth activists' own understandings of politics and
6 the political, and what they understand can be sources of meaningful
7 change to the social and political order. In each case study presented
8 here, the authors have also investigated the meaning the activists invest
9 into their actions and the bases upon which they see themselves as a
10 separate generation. The studies have also sought to make explicit the
11 political content of their practices and actions, drawing as well on the
12 notion of prefiguration and the experimentation of political ideals in
13 the means of action (Van de Sande 2013), to assess the extent to which
14 the spaces where they engage as well as their means of engagement are,
15 in fact, distinctly political in nature. By thinking of 'youth' as a distinct
16 political practice, the authors here have delved into the activists'
17 underlying shared schemata regarding what constitutes 'politics' and
18 how they qualify their own action, and how these in turn inform their
19 practices of activism. In so doing, the studies and commentaries here
20 are able to shed light on their discursive practice and use of terms such
21 as 'apolitical', on the spaces and populations with whom they choose
22 to engage, and how these represent an alternative manifestation of
23 political claims.

Investigating Youth Practice from Multiple Perspectives

26   The studies and conceptual reflections that have been brought
27 together in this collection intentionally draw on different disciplines,
28 perspectives, and linguistic scholarly traditions in an effort to put forth
29 an inclusive process of knowledge production and develop an analytical
30 concept of youth that can be translated across different fields of
31 research and praxis. Three of the chapters presented here, covering the
32 Algeria, Tunisia, and Lebanese cases, have been produced by authors
33 representing three distinct subfields in the social sciences – political
34 science, sociology, and psychology – and as such draw on different sets
35 of literature and interpretive lenses in their investigation of youth-as-
36 practice. In this way, the collection conducts both a situating of youth
37 activism and generational political practice within broader structures of

1   power and political system, but also an assessment of how social
2   identities and ecology as well as affective ties inform collective
3   schemata and competent performance. In addition to these academic
4   studies, volume also captures a distinct practitioner perspective with
5   the chapter on Syria. Written by a youth activist on her own community
6   of practice, the commentary uses an oral history approach to reveal
7   youth-as-practice by drawing forth the collective narration of recent
8   historical events. Finally, the concluding chapter, provides a broad
9   sociological reflection on what is meant by youth and how a youth
10   politics is itself embedded in social structures, political opportunities
11   and cultures, and positionality.

12   The multidisciplinary and multiple perspective nature of this
13   collection also resides in the different languages in which knowledge
14   has been produced and conveyed, allowing for a diversification in
15   scholarly voices outside the hegemony of the English-language
16   academy. Two of the studies were produced in French (the chapters
17   on Tunisia and Algeria), while the chapter on Syria commentary was
18   produced in Arabic. This use of different languages is not merely a
19   question of linguistic facility or predilection; it also pertains to the
20   epistemological manner in which one's reality is captured and the
21   codified manner in which information is relayed, ideas are constructed,
22   and arguments are elaborated that themselves represent different
23   scholarly traditions. While the works in French and Arabic have been
24   translated into English, the structures of the pieces and the manners in
25   which research is reported have remained intact in order to bring forth
26   these different codes and to resist the homogenization of academia in
27   the Anglo-American tradition. The diverse voices, perspectives, and
28   traditions that are captured in this volume have allowed for the more
29   robust development of the concept of youth but also its ability to be
30   deployed in a variety of subfields and cases.

31   In her study on civic activists in Algeria (in which the fieldwork was
32   conducted prior to the 2019 uprising, with shorter follow-up interviews
33   in spring 2019), Layla Baamara places centrally the particular contextual
34   background and the role it plays in shaping both the means and manner
35   of youth engagement. This includes the only partially applied
36   institutional reforms of 2011, whereby important obstacles and
37   constraints for associative actors continue to exist, but also the received
38   historical memory of the civil war and its ensuing impact on how these

1   youth think about politics and mobilization. Her study finds that
2   civically engaged Algerian youth (here comprised almost entirely of
3   those representing the socio-economic and educational elites) are both
4   very politicized and interested in the Aristotelian 'polis', yet do not see
5   themselves as political actors and indeed hold an aversion to what they
6   call 'politics'. As such, they deliberately distance themselves from the
7   formal political sector and expressly qualify their work as 'apolitical'.
8   Yet at the same time, they defend the idea that their civic engagement
9   aims at change, including change to the political and social context of
10   the country. Her research reveals an important duality that marks
11   Algerian youth civic engagement: it is both integrative and transgressive
12   /transformative at the same time. In this sense, there is both a
13   reproduction of norms and order as well as their breaking down. Thus
14   while youth are willing to work within the 'red lines' of acceptable
15   action as delimited by the regime as a manner of achieving social
16   integration through their action, they also see these same actions as a
17   means of transgressing the established political and social order. To
18   this point, their use of the term 'apolitical' to qualify their civic
19   engagement has double meaning. On one hand, it reflects a shared
20   understanding of politics as standing opposed to change-oriented civic
21   engagement; on the other hand, it represents a deliberate rhetorical
22   device to establish acceptability and garner support for their action.

23   In his work on activist youth in post-revolutionary Tunisia and in
24   particular their self-organization in the form of one-off campaigns and
25   rhizomatic networks, Mounir Saidani reveals a 'culturalization' and
26   globalization of political expression and the 'juvenalization' and
27   hybridization of politics that permeates youth civic engagement. This
28   includes the visual representation of political demands and the refusal
29   to include political ideologies, as well as new forms of contractual,
30   short-term, and renewable solidarities that differ from identity-based
31   or class-based solidarities that characterized social movements in the
32   past. For youth activists, such engagement not only represents a new
33   manner of 'doing' politics but also a new manner of living and of being
34   together that is non-hierarchical, non-differentiated, and that can be
35   reactivated at will. Their engagement reflects a rebuilding of their
36   society that is part of breaking down the former political and social
37   order that was produced by the State and reproduced by political
38   parties as well as traditional civil society actors. This breaking down of
39   the former political and social order also reflects a fluidity in the

1   Tunisian youth engagement. To this point, his research points to the
2   innovative modes of youth civic engagement that are themselves
3   prefiguring political goals: engaged youth in post-revolution Tunisia
4   have indeed been making a deliberate effort to develop new
5   organizational models that are horizontal, democratic, and
6   participatory, with a core/periphery structure that can weather
7   moments of abeyance.

8   Khaled Nasser's and Sarah Anne Rennick's research covering
9   youth-led NGOs, civic initiatives, and new political forces in Lebanon
10 (also carried out prior to the October 2019 Revolution) unveiled a
11 shared and distinctively political goal, that of resistance to the status
12 quo and in particular the sectarian political system and endemic
13 corruption it presents. Viewing themselves as an imagined community,
14 the Civil Society, their various forms of engagement are understood
15 both as a means of self-actualization, but also a way to fight the
16 disappointment they see within the current political context and the
17 limitations it imposes on their lives – albeit through diverse vectors that
18 range from participation in municipal elections to spreading a sense of
19 joyful national identity. Indeed, all the youth activists studied here view
20 their engagement as an act of political resistance, even if their activities
21 are not in any way linked to politics or the political sector. For them,
22 activism within the Civil Society is attempting to either directly or
23 indirectly change the sectarian elite system. Importantly, though,
24 Nasser and Rennick identify the markedly divergent effects that
25 different forms of engagement produce on the system: while some
26 actions are indeed working to alter the existing political status quo,
27 others are actually driving forth system maintenance by filling gaps in
28 State dysfunction.

29   In her oral, insider history of Syrian youth in the transition from
30 revolutionary activists to members of local councils in zones no longer
31 under regime control, Hadia Kawekji's commentary piece finds that
32 youth hold little interest in participating in politics once the war ends.
33 She reveals instead a distinct impression of lost agency that directly
34 impacts the way youth in local councils understand their political
35 action. While their work with the local councils represents ostensibly
36 local and municipal political action, they view this work as service
37 provision only, and pointedly state that the local councils are not
38 political. In their collective understanding, the 'political' is located

1   elsewhere, in the high negotiations process in Geneva and Astana, and
2   in large-scale representative institutions rather than the local level. The
3   pre-revolution fear of being labeled 'political' and the re-definition of
4   the content and location of politics and the political in light of the
5   current situation and their own loss of control over the revolutionary
6   movement coincides with an important facture between revolutionary
7   work vs. political work, in which one type of action – that promoting
8   revolutionary change – is seen as categorically different from 'politics'.

9   Finally, in his conceptual piece on the concept and elaboration of
10 'youth politics' in analytical terms, Asef Bayat argues that the quality of
11 youth is not merely tangential to political phenomenon such as the
12 Arab uprisings but rather represents a distinct politics. Exploring youth
13 in Bourdieuian terms, he argues that youth habitus is associated with
14 the sociological position of structural irresponsibility, and as such that
15 a youth politics in conceptual terms should at least in some part
16 comprise the claiming or reclaiming of the youthfulness. As he argues,
17 however, youth politics is also mediated by other factors including
18 positionality and social identity as well as political cultures and
19 opportunities. As such, youth political behavior and claims are not
20 simply limited to the expression of youthful agency but also the social
21 structures in which different identities are embedded and the broader
22 political contexts in which these operate. As he concludes, the
23 transformative nature of the Arab uprisings is thus not in itself a
24 product of youth politics per se nor a pre-supposed revolutionary
25 quality to youthfulness. Rather, Arab youth were able to act as agents
26 of radical change precisely because of their ability to bridge the
27 preoccupations of youthfulness with broader social and political claims
28 of the citizenry, finding expression in distinctly youth repertoires of
29 contention.

How Collective Understandings of 'Youth' Inform
30
31 ## Activism

32   Taken together, this volume reveals a number of important themes
33 related to how civically engaged Arab youth think about politics/the
34 political versus their own work, and how these shared understandings
35 inform the modes and means of their activism. One striking feature
36 shared across the case studies is the dichotomization of 'politics' and
37 'youth' work. Across the case studies, the youth activists interviewed

1   understand the realm of politics and the political to be limited to formal
2   and institutional instances, such as parties, parliaments, and elections
3   processes, that are ultimately designed to maintain the system status
4   quo. These are, in turn, elite-dominated and a realm of action that is
5   restricted to an older generation. Thus in Tunisia, for example, despite
6   the democratic gains following the ouster of Ben Ali in 2011, the
7   political process has been understood as elite maintenance through
8   power sharing cohabitation arrangements; in Algeria, politics is seen as
9   the institutional realm of a geriatric class that seeks to maintain a largely
10   opaque stranglehold over decision-making; and in Lebanon, politics is
11   viewed as a mechanism of distribution for the feudalistic sectarian
12   system that is a vestige of the post-civil war generation. In this way,
13   'politics' is specifically a manner of reproduction of both existing elites
14   but also the existing social and political order and the manner of
15   structuring the relationship between citizens and the State. It is also, in
16   their collective understanding, a form of participation that is supported
17   and sustained by an older generation that has benefited from system
18   maintenance. The 'political', as such, is reduced to these formal and
19   institutional instances and an underlying aim – whether implicit or
20   explicit – is to maintain the status quo. This stands in stark contrast to
21   the shared understanding of their own work. For the youth activists
22   researched here, both direct political protest as well as their diverse
23   forms of civic engagement stand in contrast to politics both because of
24   the mode of action but also its objectives and purpose. The youth
25   activists across the four case studies deliberately locate their action
26   outside of formal and institutional realms, and indeed state their strong
27   desire to develop modes of engagement that defy traditional models of
28   parties or even NGOs, which they view are susceptible to falling prey
29   to 'politics'. A defining feature of their understanding of 'youth' is
30   indeed this attempt to locate action and activism in organizational
31   realms that differ from those that are formal or institutionalized in
32   either the political sector or the civic space.

33   Perhaps more importantly, they do not identify a political
34   dimension to their civic activism precisely because they are seeking to
35   break with the status quo. Whereas their direct political protests seek
36   outwardly regime or systemic change, their civic engagement seeks
37   changes to the existing regimes of distribution, the existing divisions
38   between the included/the excluded, and the erected barriers that
39   structure social interactions. It is in fact these changes to the status quo

1   – the unfairness of distribution policies and the social injustice they
2   create, the politics of non-recognition and the absence of full
3   citizenship, the social stratification that undermines national belonging
4   and identity – that they see as the purpose of their civic activism. Yet
5   as opposed to demanding these changes directly, they understand their
6   work as enacting such changes by working around the State. In this
7   way, their qualification of their work as 'apolitical' refers specifically to
8   the collective understanding that their work is change-oriented and
9   thus must come from outside politics and the political process. It also
10   reveals their shared assumptions about the sources of meaningful
11   change: for the activists, change cannot come from top-down
12   processes or piecemeal reform movements, but instead must come
13   from forces outside those channeled by the political. Importantly, this
14   does not imply a preference for radical revolutionary action; on the
15   contrary, in both Algeria and Lebanon the activists interviewed here
16   were wary of revolutionary chaos, citing their country's own recent
17   pasts and the inherited memory of civil war as cautionary tales against
18   revolutionary instability. Yet, even their own preference for an ordered
19   process of democratic transition must necessarily come from outside
20   'politics' and top-down processes – as would be shown in 2019 with
21   the onset of revolutionary waves in both countries.

22   In addition, the research into the activists' shared understandings
23   and attributions of meaning has also revealed an understanding of
24   themselves as bearers of new national narratives that break with those
25   which buttress the current political status quo. The Algerian youth
26   activists reject the national security narratives that have been used to
27   maintain military power, for example, while the Tunisian youth activists
28   reject the backward-looking narratives of Bourguiba-era independence.
29   These new national narratives are not incidental to their activism;
30   rather, they form an important part of their self-understanding as a
31   distinct generation.

32   In conceiving of youth as a generational practice of politics, the
33   research has thus revealed that, in their quality of 'youth', these activists
34   see themselves as bearers of new national narratives, seeking equal
35   recognition, representation, and distribution, and understand that their
36   action differs in its form and modes of organization. Given this, they
37   understand that their field of action must necessarily be outside of
38   politics and is necessarily not 'political', given that its purpose is to

1   change the status quo and put forth a new national narrative and given
2   that they see the organizational dimensions of their work as being
3   distinct to their generation. In other words, the decision to remain
4   outside of politics reflects a shared belief that 'youth' work by
5   definition is not 'political', is located elsewhere, and has a different joint
6   enterprise. This manner in which the activists understand themselves
7   and their work as a separate generation informs their activism in three
8   ways.

9   First, their joint enterprise to break with the status quo and
10 specifically their aim to circumvent the current politics of distribution,
11 recognition, and social interaction, informs the sectors where youth
12 undertake civic activism and how they work with communities. More
13 precisely, youth civic engagement specifically targets fields where the
14 State is absent in order to enact their visions of fairness and inclusion.
15 This translates to work in specific sectors – the provision of social
16 services, work with excluded communities, cultural heritage protection,
17 among others. Youth civic activists working in the fields of alternative
18 urban planning, for example, choose deliberately to work in
19 neighborhoods and with local populations that are absent from the
20 State's planning radar. Likewise, youth civic activists leading
21 neighborhood clean-up activities in Beirut, or providing music facilities
22 to disadvantaged adolescents in Algiers, are expressly aiming to provide
23 services where they see the State as deficient. And because the youth
24 activists are working in the gaps where the State is absent, they are also
25 aiming to change expectations and awareness of rights among their
26 target populations. Second, the activists' collective understanding of
27 'youth' as a generational mode of work influences organizational
28 dimensions to their activism. This is not simply limited to working
29 outside traditional institutional structures but also to the methods of
30 decision-making and communications. There is a deliberate and very
31 present objective within these youth activist groups to break with the
32 hierarchies and opaque decision-making structures that they see as part
33 of an older generational way of working. Indeed, it is possible to
34 observe an experimental socialization process in democratic decision-
35 making and new forms of participation. As has been well documented
36 in the literature on youth protest movements, the youth civic activists
37 studied here also repeatedly cite the practice of 'horizontality' in their
38 collaborative work, including consensus-based decision-making,
39 shared leadership, and the encouragement of participation from all

1 members of a group. Third, youth civic activism is specifically seeking
2 to promote a new manner of being together that is based on forms of
3 social mixing that break with the normal political order. This informs
4 in particular how they work with their target groups: the youth activists
5 studied here are deliberately adopting inclusive approaches whereby
6 target groups themselves are not only beneficiaries but also are co-
7 implementers of action. This effort to privilege the skills, knowledge,
8 and ambitions of others and put forth participatory forms of collective
9 action also breaks with top-down approaches to development they
10 view as pertaining to an older generational mode of action.

Youth Civic Engagement as Alternative Form of Political Activism

13 Collectively, the pieces presented here make a strong case for
14 reconceiving of youth civic engagement in the post-2011 period as an
15 alternative form of political activism. On one hand, the underling aims
16 and objectives of this civic engagement are not only challenging the
17 political status quo but indeed are manifesting the same goals as those
18 pronounced during mass protests movements. Crucially, these various
19 forms of 'apolitical' activism are understood by the activists as a means
20 of fulfilling political demands for social justice and equal rights. The
21 link that they draw between direct political activism in the form of
22 protest movements and indirect political activism in the form of civic
23 engagement thus becomes clearer. On the other hand, the implicit
24 critique of practices of power, decision-making, and top-down
25 hierarchies that inform the activists organizational modes are largely
26 identical in both political protest movements as in civic activist
27 initiatives and groups. These are deliberate choices that are specifically
28 seeking to put forth a different practice of authority and participation
29 and that prefigure their political demands for change. To this point, it
30 is the shared intention behind these different forms of activism – to
31 challenge the existing status quo – that helps elucidate how the activists
32 themselves see their civic engagement as a continuation or alternative
33 manifestation of their political activism.

34 Yet, the potential political impact of this civic engagement as an
35 alternative form of political activism perhaps remains to be seen. Three
36 early conclusions can be drawn, all of which merit further investigation.
37 First, these forms of civic engagement seem, in certain cases, to be

1   filling governance gaps, where the State's ability to apply policies is
2   either faltering or absent. In providing services such as schooling and
3   health in zones where the State has collapsed, or by undertaking urban
4   planning and zoning enforcement in areas that are ignored by the
5   central authority, this civic activism may in fact contributing to a
6   process of 'governance from below' (El-Meehy 2017). Nowhere is this
7   more obvious than in the case of the Syrian local councils, which acted
8   as de facto local authorities where youth activists were exercising a
9   degree of political authority, including the promulgation of new
10 policies and rules. However, the degree to which these actions can
11 actually influence the State and its governance patterns remains to be
12 seen. Exploring such activism as a form of governance in areas of
13 limited statehood (Börzel, Risse, and Draude 2018) could perhaps shed
14 light on the extent to which such activism can, over time, have an
15 impact on policies and State-society relations. Second, these forms of
16 civic engagement can be conceptualized as forms of active citizenship
17 (Kaya and Bee 2017) that have the capacity to break with regimes of
18 citizenship and create new social-spatial solidarities that transcend
19 territorial and symbolic borders. One striking feature of these various
20 forms of civic engagement captured in the case studies covered here is
21 their translocal dimension: while many of the youth are carrying out
22 their activism in highly local contexts, they are doing so from places of
23 diaspora or exile where they find themselves in a liminal status of
24 citizenship, belonging neither here nor there and subject to either
25 continual surveillance by the State or rejected as outsiders. By
26 continuing their activism despite these borders and the associated
27 liminality of being without determined citizenship, the youth activists
28 are carving out a new form of political agency. The extent to which this
29 can be capitalized on in the future, either at home or indeed abroad,
30 seems a budding trend for future research. Third, this civic activism is
31 understood by the youth activists themselves as a form of abeyance
32 structure, allowing for movement maintenance between periods of
33 direct challenge on the State (Sawyers and Meyer 1999). In other words,
34 they view their civic engagement as means of maintaining their
35 engagement and networks, and continue pursuing their goals and
36 values, despite waves of demobilization, and thus as contributing to
37 future waves of political protest by allowing for a reactivation of
38 currently dormant movements. The 2019-2020 protest movements in
39 Algeria and Lebanon provide an empirical opportunity to test this

1 assumption - and to assess the extent to which a learning process is
2 taking place between different modes and waves of political activism.

3 This volume thus provides critical nuance to our understanding of
4 what constitutes political participation, and the various forms and even
5 geographies that contestation and resistance can take in the post-2011
6 period. To this point, we offer that the wave of mass protests in
7 Algeria, Sudan, Lebanon, and Iraq that started in 2019 and that are
8 struggling to continue in the context of Covid-19, State collapse, and
9 renewed oppression can perhaps be understood within terms of
10 continuity and the fluid boundaries between the civic and the political.

References

12 Abdou, Ehaab D. and Loubna H. Skalli. 2018. "Egyptian Youth-led Civil
13   Society Organizations: Alternative Spaces for Civic Engagement?" In *What*
14   *Politics? Youth and Political Engagement in Africa*, edited by Elina Oinas, Henri
15   Onodera and Leena Suurpää, 75-94, Brill Open E-Book Collection *Youth*
16   *in a Globalizing World* vol. 6.
17 Adler, Emanuel and Vincent Pouliot. 2011. "International Practices:
18   Introduction and Framework." In *International Practices*, edited by Emanuel
19   Adler and Vincent Pouliot, 1-36. Cambridge: Cambridge University Press.
20 Amara, Mahfoud. 2012. "Football Sub-Culture and Youth Politics in Algeria."
21   *Mediterranean Politics* 17, no.1: 41-58.
22 Börzel, Tanja., Thomas Risse, and Anke Draude. 2018. "Governance in Areas
23   of Limited Statehood: Conceptual Clarifications and Major Contributions
24   of the Handbook." In *The Oxford Handbook of Governance and Limited*
25   *Statehood*, edited by Tanja A. Börzel, Thomas Risse, and Anke Draude.
26   Oxford: Oxford University Press.
27 El-Meehy, Asya. 2017. "Governance from Below: Comparing Local
28   Experiments in Egypt and Syria after the Uprisings." The Century
29   Foundation. Accessed June 30, 2020. https://tcf.org/content/report/
30   governance-from-below/?agreed=1
31 Hassabo, Chaymaa. 2009. "Du rassemblement à l'effritement des Jeunes pour
32   le changement egyptiens. L'Expérience de 'générations qui ont vécu et
33   vivent toujours sous la loi d'urgence'." *Revue internationale de politique*
34   *comparée.* 16, no.20: 241-261.
35 Kaya, Ayhan and Cristiano Bee. 2017. "Youth and Active Citizenship in
36   Turkey: Engagement, Participation, and Emancipation." *Southeast European*
37   *and Black Sea Studies* 17, no.1: 129-143.
38 Korany, Bahgat and Mostafa El-Sayyed. 2107. "Youth Political Engagement
39   during the Arab Spring: Egypt and Tunisia Compared." SAHWA Scientific
40   Paper. Accessed June 30, 2020. https://www.cidob.org/en/publications/

publication_series/project_papers/sahwa_papers/scientific_paper/youth
_political_engagement_during_the_arab_spring_egypt_and_tunisia_com
pared

Lust-Okar, Ellen and Saloua Zerhouni. 2008. *Political Participation in the Middle East.* Boulder, CO: Lynne Rienner Publishers.

Mannheim, Karl. 1923. "The Problem of Generations." In *Essays on the Sociology of Knowledge,* edited by Karl Mannheim (1952). London: RKP.

Murphy, Emma C. 2012. "Problematizing Arab Youth: Generational Narratives of Systemic Failure." *Mediterranean Politics* 17, no.1: 5-22.

Onodera, Henri, Bruno Lefort, Karim Maiche, and Sofia Laine. 2020. "Dynamics of Engagement among Youth in Arab Mediterranean Countries." *Journal of North African Studies* 25, no.2: 280-303.

Onodera, Henri. 2009. "The Kifaya Generation: Politics of Change Among Youth in Egypt." *Suomen Antropologi: Journal of the Finnish Anthropological Society* 34, no.4: 44-64.

Radsch, Courtney C. 2008. "Core to Commonplace: The Evolution of Egypt's Blogosphere." *Arab Media and Society* 6, Accessed June 30, 2020. https://www.arabmediasociety.com/core-to-commonplace-the-evolution-of-egypts-blogosphere/

Sawyers, Traci M. and David S. Meyer. 1999. Missed Opportunities: Social Movement Abeyance and Public Policy. *Social Problems* 46, no.2: 187-206.

Shehata, Dina. 2010. *Youth Mobilization in Egypt: New Trends and Opportunities.* Beirut: Issam Fares Institute for Public Policy and International Affairs, American University of Beirut. Accessed June 30, 2020. https://www.aub.edu.lb/ifi/Documents/events/2012-2013/20121114ifi_youth%20mobilization%20in%20egypt_background_paper_Shehata_final.pdf

Shehata, Dina. 2008. "Youth Activism in Egypt." *Arab Reform Brief* 23, Arab Reform Initiative. Accessed June 30, 2020. https://www.arab-reform.net/publication/youth-activism-in-egypt/

Sika, Nadine. 2017. "Varieties of Youth Civic and Political Engagement in the South East Mediterranean: A Comparative Analysis." Power2Youth Working Paper no. 23. Accessed June 30, 2020. https://www.iai.it/sites/default/files/p2y_23.pdf

Van de Sande, Mathijs. 2013. "The Prefigurative Politics of Tahrir Square – An Alternative Perspective on the 2011 Revolutions." *Res Publica* 19, no.3: 223-239.

Wenger, Etienne. 1998. *Communities of Practice: Learning, Meaning and Identity.* Cambridge: Cambridge University Press.

Zerhouni, Saloua. 2017. "Explaining Youth Participation and Non-Participation in Morocco." Power2Youth Working Paper no. 36. Accessed June 30, 2020. https://www.iai.it/sites/default/files/p2y_36.pdf

YOUTH AND POLITICS IN BOUTEFLIKA'S ALGERIA: INVOLVEMENT AT A DISTANCE FROM 'POLITICS'

Layla Baamara

As mass popular mobilization emerged in Algeria on 22 February 2019, the reading of the Hirak (movement) in both the press and scholarly research were quick to describe the new 2019 as 'the year of awakening of Algerian youth.' A corollary of this common reading of ongoing events is the existence of a formerly apathetic and depoliticized youth. Prior to 22 February, journalists and observers of political life in Algeria tended to stress youth's disinterest in politics, a discourse which was echoed in political and associational spheres. In interviews carried out as recently as 2017, for example, a 31-year-old member of a local association in the *wilaya* (province) of Tlemcen commented that 'young people couldn't care less about politics' while the director of an association for environmental protection in the east of the country said with regret, 'young people are not sufficiently politicized. There's a widespread couldn't-care-less attitude, they are resigned, it's a pity' (Anonymous interviews with author, 2017).

Yet, from his first term as president, Abdelaziz Bouteflika experienced a vast wave of protest, spearheaded by youth: on 14 June 2011 tens of thousands demonstrated in Algiers in protests that were violently suppressed.[1] And again in January 2011, it was Algerian youth who made headlines in the international press alongside their Tunisian counterparts. Some weeks later, on 12 April, students defied the ban on street demonstrations and protested in the capital in their thousands. More recently, in 2018, resident doctors mobilized for several months in Algerian public spaces, relying in particular on the tactic of sit-ins. Indeed, an exhaustive analysis of youth protests in Algeria is almost impossible given the number and recurrent nature of such events. Broadly speaking, it is mainly young people who are out on the streets throughout Algeria, protesting regularly — violently or

---

[1] Following this protest, a decree was issued banning marches and gatherings in public places in Algiers. The several months of protests left 127 dead.

1   peacefully, in an organised way or spontaneously, in ongoing or adhoc
2   fashion — against government policies. And Algerian youth are
3   particularly active in the universities where they regularly express their
4   political discontent, while the associational milieu is largely populated
5   by young people who are actively investing in society at the local level.
6   In short, despite coercive policies, reforms, and income redistribution
7   introduced by government to defuse protest, Algerian youth are
8   anything but apathetic.

9   Without denying or minimizing the upheavals observed in the
10   protests of the 2019 Hirak — which I will return to briefly in the
11   conclusion — this article focuses on placing the analysis of young
12   people's relation with politics in Algeria in a longer timeframe. Starting
13   from fieldwork carried out closely with actors over a ten-year period
14   and specifically based on a qualitative survey carried out in 2017 of
15   young people involved in civil society associations, I illustrate the force
16   of ongoing mobilization. The survey produced important empirical
17   data: 24 qualitative interviews with young people aged 20–36 who are
18   members of associations in the cities of Algiers, Oran, Tlemcen, Sidi-
19   Bel-Abbès, Blida, Constantine, Skikda, Hassi Messaoud and Ouergla.[2]
20   From this research, two main — yet paradoxical — findings emerge:
21   on the one hand, youth are keen to keep a distance from politics, and
22   on the other hand, they are actively engaged 'to change things' in the
23   political sense.

24   The main thesis defended here illustrates that an avoidance of
25   politics must not be interpreted as an indication of apathy, being
26   apolitical, or a disinterest in politics. On the contrary, we can observe
27   consensus on the generalized disrepute of established politics and a
28   shared critical vision of party actors and governments in office. We also
29   observe ordinary forms of politicization in enterprises whose aim is to
30   compensate the absence or inadequacy of the State, particularly
31   regarding programs or structures destined for the young and discourse
32   expressing a desire for change. My central argument is to emphasize
33   how these forms of alternative engagement, labelled 'apolitical' by
34   some young people, are in fact a vector not only of social integration
35   but also of the transgression of the established political order.

---

[2] Interviews lasted between 45 minutes and 2 hours 30 minutes. Most interviews were recorded
with the interviewee's consent. Among the 24 interviews, four were collective, with two or more
people present.

1   Rather than reifying the discourse of these actors, our observations
2   and in-depth interviews allow us to understand how the presumed
3   'apoliticism' of some young people is part of the process of 'defining
4   situations' (Goffman 1959; Blumer 1969). 'Apolitical' can mean
5   rejecting the 'intrusion of preoccupations and goals related to politics'
6   (Lagroye 2003, 365), thereby dissociating from actors taking part in the
7   institutionalized political game or actors who have incorporated the
8   socially discredited but largely shared nature of politics and the formal
9   sphere of the political.

10   To understand their relations with politics and the engagement of
11   young people during the period 2010-2019, this article is organized in
12   four parts. First, I address their place in the protests of 2011 when
13   several countries in the region experienced large-scale popular
14   uprisings; then I outline the constraints that limit their opportunities to
15   act in the public sphere. This is followed by an assessment of the
16   different types of engagement observed despite the restrictive and
17   deterrent context. The last part is devoted to an analysis of the origins
18   and forms of discourse on politics expressed by the youth interviewees.

Youth in 2011: Protest as Socialization in Political Involvement

19
20

21   In 2011, while Tunisia and Egypt were undergoing serious popular
22   uprisings that destabilized their ruling coalitions, Algeria was generally
23   classified among the countries where the 'wave' of revolutions had
24   collided with the coercive and reform-oriented reactions of a regime
25   that remained intact despite repeated protest. Redistributive measures,
26   planned reforms, the memory of the civil war, and the fear of dispersed
27   leadership are some of the most frequently cited responses explaining
28   the absence of a popular uprising in Algeria. The mix of a dose of
29   freedoms (party pluralism, press independence, regular elections)
30   alongside a dose of coercion and monopolization of resources, expertly
31   managed by those in power, certainly helped deter protest. Although
32   useful for understanding the situation, these elements tend to make us
33   forget the mobilization that mushroomed in the first six months of
34   2011.

35   Early in January 2011, in response to a sharp hike in the prices of

1   sugar and oil,[3] thousands of young Algerians expressed their discontent
2   on the streets of the country's main cities. This in turn led to the
3   damage of public and private goods, but above all it gave rise to brutal
4   clashes with the police. Before the Tunisian president resigned, the five
5   dead, along with the wounded and those arrested after clashes between
6   rioters and police, led to widespread indignation. And although not
7   new, the protest was of such scope that events moved fast.
8   Nonetheless, the use of repressive mechanisms and the temporary
9   lifting of some taxes (customs duties, VAT, corporate income tax)
10   allowed the government to rapidly contain the protests. Yet despite this
11   containment, we can observe a proliferation of protest mobilization.

12   Indeed, while the state of emergency was still in force and street
13   demonstrations were still officially banned in Algiers,[4] for some
14   months the capital lived in the midst of rallies, sit-ins, strikes, and
15   marches of angry citizens. Most mobilization related to the targeted
16   demands of specific professional sectors (lawyers, doctors, textile
17   workers, teachers, office workers etc.). Students made their voices
18   heard in reaction to a decree that would reorganize the system of
19   college degrees (Baamara 2013) while other initiatives openly called for
20   change and the removal of those in power.[5] The enthusiasm and
21   excitement that characterized this occupation of Algerian public space
22   contrasted with the routine modes of mobilization, and became
23   synonymous for many actors with new possibilities for action.

24   In 2011 young people were not only at the forefront of these public
25   events, they also organized protest collectives—based on the
26   Mouvement des Jeunes Indépendants pour le Changement (MJIC)—
27   and mobilized in independent student committees. Assessing these
28   different expressions of contestation necessitates going beyond the
29   analytical confines of the 'Arab Spring,' requiring distance from the
30   revolutionary temporality of other national situations. It is by
31   anchoring these protests observed in the history of Algerian since the
32   end of the civil war and the Kabyle citizens' movement in the early

---

[3] According to the *Office national des statistiques* (ONS), the price of sugar and oil increased by 25% and 17% respectively in December 2010 compared to December 2009.

[4] The government banned peaceful marches and all other forms of public protest in Algiers. The lifting of the state of emergency on 23 February 2011 did not remove this ban.

[5] The *Coordination nationale pour le changement et la démocratie* (CNCD), covers trade unions, associations, political parties and unlicensed collectives which called for many of the marches (Baamara, 2012).

1 2000s that we can understand what has changed and what remains
2 conventional.

3   Yet, while the mobilization of 2011 was innovative in terms of form,
4 it nonetheless did not disrupt the established order of protest practices.
5 Here it is essential to mention that the old cleavages among mobilized
6 groups persisted and that the challenge to the regime was not
7 composed of a shared demand. Although young people engaged in
8 protest, some avoided expressing explicitly political demands, meaning
9 those aimed directly at the government in office, while others preferred
10 to remain separate from political protest altogether. In particular, the
11 absence of prior activist socialization and the fear of tipping into the
12 sort of chaos associated with the civil war in the 1990, along with the
13 situation in neighboring Libya, all contributed to this distance with
14 protest mobilization. In fact, the difference between ordinary citizens
15 and activist citizens reveals the persistence of classical structures of
16 mobilization in Algeria that only stretch marginally beyond those actors
17 already involved. However, far from inducing support for government,
18 this distance accommodated the critical discourse of the existing order.
19 The apparent 'apoliticism,' which often reinforces the thesis of political
20 apathy of the dominated in an authoritarian situation, is more in line
21 with the negative connotation of the political field and of groups
22 carrying political discourse - including therefore those claiming to be
23 opposition and/or acting outside the political field.

24   Both the forms and the limitations of mobilization in 2011 highlight
25 the relation to protest and, more broadly, to politics in Algeria,
26 particularly among youth. If this episode of protest in the context of
27 the 'Arab Spring' has been experienced by most young people and
28 comes across in 2011 as a distinct moment of socialization in political
29 involvement and activism, it does not appear to be a determining factor
30 in the experiences related by the youth interviewed in 2017. To
31 understand the modes and domains of their engagement, it is
32 important to have a broader understanding of the political and social
33 context in which they had developed.

34 ## An Inauspicious Context for Engagement

35   The Algerian government undertook a series of reforms in response
36 to the 2011 protests. On 15 April, President Abdelaziz Bouteflika
37 announced that the Constitution would be amended and that reforms

1   were planned, particularly on electoral law and political parties.[6] These
2   measures were adopted several months later but did not overturn the
3   rules of the political game. Instead they lead to the formal approval of
4   new party organizations as of January 2012. For the associational
5   sector, the freedom of association law adopted in 1990 was not
6   formally challenged after the interruption of the electoral process of
7   1991. The post-war context and post-11 September 2001 favoured the
8   development of private and interstate enterprises to promote 'civil
9   society' and, thus, to contain political Islam. Thanks to their ability to
10   compensate for a State 'in retreat' and to offer an alternative to
11   'Islamist' associations, many associations were financed by
12   international aid and became part of the international network of
13   cooperation and development aid.

14   However, the unwieldiness and impenetrable nature of bureaucratic
15   procedures, arbitrary decisions banning, for example, meetings or
16   activities as well as the instrumentalization and cooptation of many
17   associations by the State all constitute key constraints for associational
18   actors. Indeed, coercion cannot be summed up as the use of force but
19   must be considered as part of a system of global constraint designed to
20   discourage protest and to perpetuate an established authoritarian
21   order.[7] Thus the 2012 law on associations has been particularly
22   contested by many associational actors for the additional restrictions
23   that it contains. A group of etiological associations—including the
24   Ligue Algérienne de Défense des Droits de l'Homme, the Algerian
25   section of Amnesty International and the Rassemblement Actions
26   Jeunesse (RAJ)—denounced the 'reinforcing government control of
27   the creation of associations,' 'the penalization of freedom of
28   association,' and a 'liberticidal law' (Euromed Rights 2015). For
29   example this law introduced an obligation for associations to obtain
30   prior authorization from the State. It also cut their chances of funding
31   by imposing regulations for donations and legacies from foreign

---

[6] The promised reforms dealt, in particular, with the electoral system, associations, political parties and information. Implementation started in late 2011. Upstream, general assemblies of civil society were organised on 14-16 June 2011 by the *Conseil national économique et social* (CNES) to, in President Bouteflika's words, 'free the voice of civil society within the context of a new system of governance' (for more see Dris-Aït Hamadouche 2012, Dris-Aït Hamadouche and Dris, 2012).

[7] This includes forms of open repression (preventive arrest, arrests similar to kidnappings, breaking up meetings by brutally dispersing and isolating demonstrators—even when they are very few of them, etc.), kittling or corralling, and less visible forms of repression such as control, surveillance, or infiltration which help create a general atmosphere of suspicion and an almost omnipresent threat (see Earl 2003).

1   associations in 'duly established cooperation agreements.' Prior
2   permission was also necessary for partnerships with foreign
3   associations and NGOs. The *modus operandi* of these organizations on
4   Algerian soil is also strongly framed in terms of funding opportunities
5   and the goals they may pursue.[8] Lastly, the methods of suspending or
6   disbanding associations tend to reinforce state control of the
7   associative sector. An association can, for example, be suspended or
8   disbanded by a simple bureaucratic decision 'in cases of interference in
9   the internal affairs of the country or of attack on national sovereignty.'[9]
10   In these conditions, the actors involved have problems organizing
11   themselves, enlisting members, establishing themselves socially, having
12   a voice in local politics and media, and continuing their activism despite
13   these constraints. Irrespective of all this, collectives persist, and new
14   social and cultural citizen initiatives emerge and are particularly backed
15   by youth.

16   These people, and those interviewed, focussed on difficulties linked
17   to these constraints. On the administrative and legal level, many
18   emphasize the time taken to obtain a licence to operate. This can take
19   from some months to several years, and the time that elapses from
20   submitting an application to receiving authorization is variable and
21   uncertain. In the country, associations in Algeria suffer the longest
22   delays. One had still not obtained approval after an application was
23   submitted in 2014. Manel[10] (30 years), an active member of an
24   association in Algiers which obtained formal authorization after over a
25   year's delay, explains the bureaucratic embroilment which it faced:

26   For an entire a year I ran around from one office to another...
27   I was literally turning cartwheels... I can't tell you just how
28   crazy it was...! I'm not exaggerating! Just how slow it was...
29   The fact that the State decides who to help or not, of course...
30   you help the people who help you, who can guarantee your
31   promotion, who can bring in votes or something like that [...]
32   When they saw our statutes, they told us that we couldn't have
33   empty lines between the articles because something could be
34   inserted between them...! So, they tell you to re-convene a
35   general assembly, to remove the spaces. Then, the objectives,

---

[8] Articles 63, 65 and 67 of Law 12-06.
[9] Article 39 of Law 12-06.
[10] All first names have been changed.

1   we had tried to make them very broad. Then they told me that
2   you can't call the association 'center' since 'center' means
3   'national' or it's a provincial association. No one told me
4   before! [...] In fact, it took the intervention of the *wali*
5   (provincial governor), who we met during an event, to unblock
6   things. And when the *wali* called the *daïra* (district) it went really
7   fast! We got our licence and we got premises too!

8   Faced with the slowness, uncertainty, and lack of transparency of
9   administrative procedures, young people involved in associations adapt
10   to rules by trying to enlist the help of someone in charge, such as by
11   submitting a request for authorization in another *wilaya* known to work
12   faster. Generally, the terms 'bureaucracy,' 'corruption' and 'abuse of
13   power' crop up repeatedly in the interviews to describe the role of
14   administrative and political institutions.

15   The other type of constraint most often evoked regards funding.
16   The majority of those interviewed emphasize the problem of financing
17   their activities. For example, Anis (28 years) is responsible for a local
18   association in Oran and claims that:

19   The problem is funding. We can't do anything without money.
20   All we can do is to make plans. But without money, we can't.
21   There are some public subsidies but it's virtually nothing or it
22   doesn't go to the right people.

23   In addition to a lack of public financing there is also the unequal
24   and unclear allocation of resources indicated by most interviewees.
25   Lyes (30 years), a member of a local association in Blida, observes:

26   The recreation center doesn't run activities any more. It's not
27   normal that it's empty all the time. You've seen it, there's no
28   one there while young people lack space! The youth center's a
29   business: we want consideration. For example to encourage
30   young people to go and vote.

31   Faced with the weakness and uncertainty of public funding, young
32   people are turning to sponsorship with by businesses and calls for
33   projects by international donors. A great deal is also achieved by simply
34   'being creative' in order to obtain free premises, means of transport, or
35   other material.

36   Another element stressed by most interviewees is linked to the

1　difficulty of mobilizing fellow citizens and of being sustainably
2　anchored in society. Again, Anis, cited *supra,* explains for example:

3　　　Another blockage is the engagement of the young. It may be
4　　　necessary to work on awareness. In Algeria the public image of
5　　　the associational sphere is bad... I don't know, but it's certainly
6　　　linked to the situation in the country. This could be linked to
7　　　young people themselves. You can't change things if people
8　　　themselves don't want to change.

9　　In addition to bureaucratic and legal constraints, respondents note
10　that associations can be perceived negatively or, like Manel states, that
11　they are considered 'powerless, unable to change things.' Several insist
12　more widely on the deterioration of social and economic conditions in
13　Algeria, which particularly affects the young. For Malik (26 years)
14　working for an NGO and member of a local association in Algiers, one
15　of the problems to mobilize and recruit is linked to the fact that 'young
16　people's main concern is to find work and get married.'

17　　In addition to these bureaucratic constraints at the associational
18　level, civic and political engagement of Algerian youth is also limited
19　with the parameters of socioeconomic challenges. Despite the
20　increased uptake of secondary education and the extension of
21　compulsory schooling, young people in Algeria are particularly hard hit
22　by unemployment.[11] It takes a long time to find housing and to marry,
23　irrespective of social background. In Algeria like other countries in the
24　region, pre-adulthood now lasts longer (Bonnefoy and Catusse 2013,
25　16). After the *hittistes* — derived from the Algerian Arabic word for
26　'wall,' an expression describing youth without work who 'prop up the
27　neighborhood walls' (Le Pape 2012) — come the *harragas* who burn
28　their identity papers and risk the dangerous sea crossing for exile in
29　Europe. Thus, when it is not delinquency, disturbances, or clandestine
30　emigration, it is visa applications or education abroad that are the
31　topical issues of interest for Algerian youth. The lack of interest in
32　politics and electoral abstention, which are considered particularly
33　widespread among the young, should be viewed within this context.
34　Yet, while these phenomena reveal the difficulties of social and
35　economic integration and are characteristic of Algerian youth in the
36　early 21st century, they should not conceal the range of forms of

---

[11] In 2011 the under-30s accounted for 57.7% of the total population according to official statistics.

1   involvement of young people observable in public space.

'Doing Something for Society:' Alternative Forms of Involvement

4   Perhaps somewhat paradoxically, the civil war in the 1990s, the
5   shortage of structures for youth, the problem of finding work, and the
6   lack of places to socialize are all motors of associational engagement.
7   Ahcène (30 years), a manager in a public enterprise and active in an
8   association in Algiers, explains that 'faced with the desperation among
9   the young' there is 'the desire and the need to do something positive
10   for society.' It is in order to remedy inequality in access to work that
11   young members of the Association pour le Développement des
12   Capacités des Etudiants in Oran have created their own collective: '"we
13   want to help young people [...], to change things at our level. We can
14   do a lot of things despite the constraints that already exist. We can
15   make progress, prepare, create things.' For Youssef, member of a
16   district association in Bab-Ezzouar (*wilaya* of Algiers):

17   Getting involved in this association was a way to deal with our
18   problems, with what we put up with in daily lives in our
19   country. Associations give young people a chance to get off
20   drugs, unemployment, etc.

21   Combatting social exclusion and inequalities can thus take the form
22   of associational engagement. In a context where political space is
23   heavily discredited, especially among youth, participation in an
24   association of social, cultural or artistic nature is presented as a
25   different way to be involved.

26   Most youth activists interviewed came from the middle classes.
27   They were often undergraduates or freshly graduated who had had
28   their first experience of political involvement at university or in one of
29   the prestigious *grandes écoles* and/or active in study clubs. Several of
30   them had completed internships or trainings abroad, in Europe or
31   North America. Although not in the majority in our sample,[12] other
32   respondents belong to more modest social backgrounds, namely the
33   poor with little or no higher education. Although this research is not
34   an exhaustive analysis of forms of associational involvement

---

[12] The interviews were carried out using a qualitative inductive approach without any claim to being representative.

1 observable among youth in Bouteflika's Algeria, it is nonetheless
2 possible to distinguish schematically between four types of association
3 based on the data collected and differentiate between the different
4 objectives articulated, practices described, and spaces of action targeted
5 by the surveys.

6   First are associations are engaged in promoting active citizenship of
7 the young and in defending human rights, such as the Rassemblement
8 Actions Jeunesse (RAJ), a national association set up in 1993 and
9 known for its opposition to the government in office. The members of
10 this association are openly critical of those running the country and
11 demonstrate regularly in public. Most members have had prior
12 experience of mobilization (rallies, demonstrations) and some have
13 experienced acts of repression (arrests, beatings, intimidation, etc.).
14 This association is fully integrated in Algeria's oppositional space. Since
15 its creation, it acts in concert with other actors such as independent
16 trade unions[13] or the Ligue Algérienne de Défense des Droits de
17 l'Homme (LADDH). Most members are sympathizers or members of
18 opposition political parties. The seniority of RAJ and its history of
19 activism since the 1990s contribute to its solid integration in networks
20 of transnational associations. For example, RAJ members take part in
21 global Social Forum and interact with organizations in other countries,
22 mainly in Europe and the Maghreb.

23   Second are associations anchored locally, at the town or district
24 level, that focus on social and cultural targets such as entertainment for
25 children in hospitals, aid for populations in need, or environmental
26 protection. Among these are the association of Jeunes Amis de
27 lEenvironnement in the *wilaya* of Tlemcen, in North-East Algeria,
28 whose members organise local clean-up campaigns and teach
29 awareness on environmental issues in primary schools. These
30 associations have problems when it comes to funding and other
31 resources; they are less well integrated in the network of cooperation
32 and have less resources to respond to calls for projects by financial
33 donors. However, this type of association can benefit indirectly from
34 resources obtained from other associations better embedded in donor

---

[13] The trade unions described as 'autonomous' are professional sectoral organisations that are not part of the Union Générale des Travailleurs Algériens (UGTA), the FLN's original 'mass organisation' under the single-party system and sole intersectoral confederation associated with devices for bipartisan interaction with government and tripartite interaction with, in addition, employers' organisations, despite the adoption of trade union pluralism in 1990.

1　networks. Thus, a member of one association reported having taken
2　part in a communications training course run by the association Oran
3　Intégrée as part of a programme of cooperation with the French
4　Embassy. Generally speaking, associations are able to take up calls for
5　projects or subsidies — often put forward by the French or US
6　embassies or the EU — for events (seminars, conferences, training,
7　etc.) to which other associations are invited.

8　　Third are associations that promote culture and the arts, whose
9　members use artistic means of expressing their engagement. The
10　Drôles Madaires, for example, is a troupe of youth actors from Oran
11　who promote theatrical improvisation. Associational activism has
12　become a way to pursue an artistic trajectory or to give free expression
13　to a hobby. In addition to organizing performances, the Drôles
14　Madaires propose weekly beginner workshops in theatrical
15　improvisation for children and adults. They also operate outside Oran
16　to meet the call of associations in other parts of Algeria to organize
17　'discovery workshops' and to perform abroad. They also take part in
18　meetings at the regional scale (Africa/Middle East) in the framework
19　of which they dialog with artists from other countries and aspire to
20　create a transnational network to promote theatrical improvisation.
21　Other young people relate more to placing their involvement at the
22　service of their passion or artistic vocation and for the benefit of other
23　young artists. This is, for example, the case of the association Jeunes
24　Talents, Jeune Espoir in Oran whose mission is to help young people
25　interested in cultural and artistic careers (also financed within the
26　framework of cooperation between the EU and Algeria).

27　　Fourth are associations that champion the social and solidarity
28　economy and social entrepreneurship. For example, the Centre
29　Algérien pour l'Entrepreneuriat Social was set up by a group of
30　students in 2013 to create enterprises with a social impact. Those who
31　have set up an enterprise or an association affirm their desire to provide
32　solutions for local social problems. These young actors are often
33　graduates from the *grandes écoles* (commerce, IT) and, even more than
34　in other types of association, they bring professional experience or have
35　been trained in Europe or the US. Their domain of activity is confined
36　to the local level and includes professional training to help launch
37　platforms for 'social' associations through the development of
38　sustainable tourism or digital inclusion. Often evoking practices and

1   actors the solidarity economy in the countries of the global North, they
2   promote the emergence of a similar sector in Algeria to respond to
3   social and economic needs inadequately met by the State. Through this
4   type of activism, youth also advocate social entrepreneurship in order
5   to try and gain entry to the labor market. Finally, their ambitions
6   resonate with the emergence of the new discourse of international
7   donors and public actors in Algeria which promote social
8   entrepreneurship as a lever of development and offer prospects of
9   funding in this perspective.

10   Thus, the participation of Algerian youth in the public domain can
11   take different forms.[14] Some claim they want to keep a distance from
12   politics while others criticize the government openly. However, this
13   does not prevent them from establishing partnerships locally with
14   public actors to obtain funding. The representations of politics
15   expressed by youth respondents are heterogeneous, but a common
16   trend emerges regarding the rejection of institutionalized politics.

Involvement Far Away from 'Politics?'

18   For the researcher entering the field, studying the representation of
19   the political starts from face-to-face interactions with local actors. In
20   the presence of a political scientist, and learning about my object of
21   inquiry, some of the youth encountered during fieldwork have
22   performed disinterest in and ignorance about the subject: 'Politics... I'm
23   not interested, it's too complicated,' 'Politics, forget it! I have nothing
24   to say about it! I don't feel concerned... not at all!' The political sphere
25   is explicitly or implicitly depicted as distinct and distant from everyday
26   life. However, such representation should not be interpreted as a form
27   of ignorance; rather, a feeling of inadequacy is a better explanation of
28   this avoidance. Political questions are deemed inaccurate, and youth
29   who express such statements somehow feels that their opinion is
30   irrelevant.

31   Indeed, talking about politics is rooted in implicit knowledge about

---

[14] We can add another category not documented here: the autonomous student committees. These are distinct from the student organisations affiliated to dominant political parties active in the political game (FLN, RND, MSP). The autonomous committees have a trade union style of operation, and defend students' rights particularly the teaching programme (organisation of courses of study and graduate degrees, available means, etc.) and social conditions (student housing, catering, etc.). They are organised horizontally and sometimes act in coordination at the national level, they are at the forefront of student protest.

1   what is deemed pronounceable and what is not, depending on the
2   circumstances. I argue that dominant norms are re-appropriated by
3   youth activists in order to express political claims. Some activists avoid
4   politics-as-label but still claim their interest in what they call "social"
5   questions. This discursive positioning of Algerian students is a case in
6   point: the apparent detachment of political considerations does not
7   mean that the activists consider their action as apolitical, but rather that
8   they act as if they did (Wedeen 1998). If they want to be heard at the
9   level of the institutional sphere, legitimate rhetoric implies making use
10   of apolitical arguments (Vairel and Zaki 2011). This differentiation
11   between political and socio-economic issues appears both excessive
12   and artificial.

13   Beyond the question of enculturation of a normalized language,
14   avoiding politics seems revealing of a rejection of institutionalized
15   politics and an adaptation to a socially shared depoliticized order. In
16   other words, the apparent rejection of the 'political' is actually linked
17   to the discredit of the institutionalized political field and results in
18   strategic use of apolitical claims. Kader (30 years), a member of an
19   environmental association in Remchi-Tlemcen, explains for example:

20   We want to remain far from politics because if we are linked
21   somehow with politicians, we are immediately toast. We lose
22   our credit and people don't trust us anymore. They would say
23   that we don't act for a good cause but to play politics.
24   Politicians don't work for society but for their own interest.

25   An extract from an interview with a member of Association
26   Culturelle de Développement des Capacités des Etudiants (ADCE) in
27   Oran is also indicative of this strategic rejection of politics that is
28   entrenched in a shared notion of a discredited political sphere:

29   We don't want to be involved in politics because when you get
30   close to politics there are always problems. We are really
31   apolitical. [...] Our image is an image of young working people.
32   We are under 30 years old. This is what makes us a success. If
33   we start to get closer to politics, it'll tarnish our image a bit. [...]
34   It won't [get us] anything and then there's the risk to our
35   credibility. [...] The Algerian political field is fuzzy. It's best to
36   avoid it.

37   Indeed, avoiding politics is not only a means to distance themselves

1   from other actors, it is also a manner to adapt to a socially shared
2   depoliticized order. Talking about 'social' problems enables the actors
3   to be perceived as if they really care about issues which affect people,
4   contrary to politicians, including those from the opposition and, to
5   distinguish themselves from self-claimed political actors. Thus, as they
6   put forward the non-political aspect of engagement or action, youth
7   activists meanwhile express a political position. Their choice of
8   apolitical speech sheds crucial light on their relationship to the political,
9   which is not reducible to its instrumental dimension. It reveals a
10 rejection of institutional politics.

11   This rejection is also linked to perceptions and experiences of a gap
12 between what young people aspire to and their place in society and,
13 more specifically, in political space. As on interviewee states: 'You're
14 left on the side, we're not even considered. [...] The institutions are full
15 of old men. It's a generational problem: they don't understand us.'

16   Most youth interviewed here also express their negative experiences
17 with political actors at moments of elections. For Kader, 'politics
18 stinks, it's rotten inside. Before elections, parties come to see us
19 because of the lists, but they don't convince us.' Sofiane (22 years), an
20 active member of an environmental association in Sidi-Bel-Abbès,
21 reports having been 'sought out by political parties' but that 'they're all
22 the same [...] you see them during the campaign because they need
23 young people but afterwards we become invisible again!' In Oran, the
24 young members of ADCE state: 'When setting things up, a party
25 representative came along, she was nice, she stayed a bit. After the
26 elections, she simply forgot the association. We're young but we're not
27 stupid.'

28   This apparently 'apolitical' involvement of the youth interviewed for
29 this study in no way implies support for political actors or the regime
30 in office. On the contrary, by labelling their forms of civic engagement
31 or mobilization as apolitical, they are — paradoxically — expressing a
32 political position that rejects the system as it stands. Indeed, the
33 relationship with politics of youth active in associations has a
34 predominantly transgressive dimension. My fieldwork confirms the
35 need to go beyond the observation of actions declared as political in
36 order to understand the political. Coercion certainly compels activists
37 to invent discrete, informal, and less obvious forms of action. Yet,
38 some forms of action and speech — here, those which are considered

1   political —are also avoided simply because it is normal to avoid them.

2   The avoiding of 'politics' is also a reflection of a general fear of
3   'chaos' as ingrained from memories of the 1990s civil war. As one
4   activist stated, 'Change will happen thanks to a long-term work. Radical
5   change is not good. We saw what happened in Libya and in Syria.'
6   Indeed, the memory of the civil war seems to have deeply affected
7   some youth actors, individually or collectively; this trauma seems to
8   account, at least in part, for their seeming preference for the political
9   status quo or at least a certain rejection of revolutionary pathways for
10   change. This is not to imply that the youth who were affected by war
11   fully endorse the government's policies, nor that they consider this
12   government to be legitimate. However, the fact that the war followed
13   the October 1988 revolt and period of political pluralism (1989-1992)
14   may help explain their skepticism towards political change. In the eyes
15   of many youth activists, preventing a replay of such tragic events is of
16   utmost importance. As such, political mobilization is sometimes
17   viewed as a potential risk that must be avoided in order not to re-live
18   the years of terror. Indeed, references to suffering, fear, and victims are
19   often mentioned as a reminder that politics has already 'made the
20   country suffer' and that the Algerian people need peace - de facto
21   requiring the maintenance of distance from politics. To this point,
22   some interviews go as far as to lay emphasis on the fact that since this
23   period, the political has been considered irrelevant and potentially
24   dangerous. This collective memory helps to explain why some
25   interviewees assert they are 'afraid of non-pacific change,' as cited by a
26   youth member of an artistic association in Constantine. Indeed, the
27   horizon for meaningful political change is for many quite long, with
28   some citing that it will not happen before ten years 'or even two
29   centuries. What we do now, it's for future generations' one interviewee
30   explains.

31   Yet despite this When they express a drive for change or challenge
32   dominant social norms, our young interviewees are, in their discourse
33   and actions, primarily opting for a way to integrate into society. When
34   they protest on the street or mobilise in associations, this is
35   notwithstanding restrictive laws, difficult social and economic
36   conditions and a lack of funding. Young Algerians want to be heard
37   and to testify to their aspiration to occupy a place in the public domain.
38   On the whole, we need to consider the dual—integrative and

1   transgressive—dimension of youth activism. The speeches and actions
2   of the young activists interviewed reveal their dissatisfaction with the
3   current political situation and how they consider their involvement as
4   a way to do something for their country and to carve out a place for
5   themselves in society.

6   *

7   The points made in this article help us to understand the Hirak and
8   sort of mobilization that has built up and consolidated after February
9   2019. The protest is exceptional in terms of its scale, regularity, and
10   diffusion throughout Algeria. It is also exceptional for its interclass and
11   intergenerational dimension, [two] forms of dissent favoured by the
12   young, dissenting Algerians. Men and women from different social
13   backgrounds, students and the unemployed, the previously [politically]
14   engaged [and the previously politically inactive], young people who
15   demonstrated in the Hirak, share—as with all the social categories
16   mobilised—a desire to put an end to the current political 'system' and
17   to introduce radical political change. Without ending up in an reading
18   of events, the present mobilisation confirms the need to abandon the
19   thesis of the apathy of subjects in an authoritarian state and to study
20   relations with politics that go beyond established political domain.

21   By way of conclusion, and based on fieldwork carried out in Algiers
22   in March and April 2019, we can make two observations: on the one
23   hand, young people already involved in associations, whether they
24   protest overtly or not, present their opposition and their involvement
25   in protest as an integral part of their own previous [social and political]
26   socialisation. If there is a discontinuity, it is not so much in the way that
27   they depict the political game as in the expressions used to articulate
28   their rejection of it. On the other hand, statements made by young
29   interviewees not previously involved in political protest attest to a
30   rejection of the political system in place before the build-up of protest
31   in 2019. In short, the discrediting and rejection of established politics
32   predates 2019. By contrast, the ways in which this rejection is expressed
33   and the perceptions of the public domain of possible action are
34   unprecedented in Algerian history. In order to have a better
35   understanding of the particular [and dual] nature of the mobilisation in
36   2019 we need to entrench the analysis of mobilization over a longer
37   period of time/over a longer period of political socialisation.

References

Baamara, Layla. 2013. "À SOS Bab-el-Oued: Rappeurs et rockeurs entre intégration et transgression à Alger." In *Jeunesses Arabes: Du Maroc au Yémen: Loisirs, Cultures, et Politiques* edited by Laurent Bonnefoy and Myriam Catusse, 230-239. Paris: La Découverte.

Baamara, Layla. 2012. "(Més)aventures d'une coalition contestataire : le cas de la Coordination nationale pour le changement et la démocratie (CNCD) en Algérie." In *L'Année du Maghreb*, 161-179. Paris: CNRS Editions.

Dris-Aït Hamadouche, Louisa. 2012. "L'Algérie face au 'printemps arabe:' l'équilibre par la neutralisation des contestations." *Confluences Méditerranée* 2, no. 81: 55-67.

Dris-Aït Hamadouche, Lousa and Chérif Dris. 201. "De la résilience des régimes autoritaires: la complexité algérienne." In *L'Année du Maghreb*, 279-301. Paris: CNRS Editions.

Earl, Jennifer. 2003. "Tanks, Tear Gas, and Taxes: Toward a Theory of Movement Repression." *Sociological Theory* 21, no. 1: 44-68.

Euromed Rights. 2015. "Memorandum: Analyse de la Loi N°12-06 du 12 Janvier 2012 Relative aux Lois sur les Associations." Accessed 01 July 2020. https://euromedrights.org/fr/publication/memorandum-analyse-de-la-loi-no12-06-du-12-janvier-2012-relative-aux-lois-sur-les-associations/

Le Pape, Loïc. 2012. "Histoire de voir le temps passer. Les hittistes algériens." In *Jeunesses Arabes: Du Maroc au Yémen: Loisirs, Cultures, et Politiques* edited by Laurent Bonnefoy and Myriam Catusse, 42-52. Paris: La Découverte.

Vairel, Frédéric and Lamia Zaki. 2011. "Politisation sous contrainte et politisation de la contrainte : outsiders politiques et outsiders de la ville au Maroc." *Critique Internationale* 50, no. 1: 91-108.

Wedeen, Lisa. 1998, "Acting 'As If': Symbolic Politics and Social Control in Syria." *Comparative Studies in Society and History* 40, no. 3: 503-523

HYBRID, CULTURE-BASED, AND YOUTHFUL: THE NEW POLITICAL COMMITMENT OF YOUTH IN POST-REVOLUTIONARY TUNISIA

Mounir Saidani

In the last year of Ben Ali's reign, pre-revolutionary Tunisia was officially proclaimed the 'Year of Youth,' with the politicians then in office once again putting forward political slogans focusing on a rapprochement with young people. As part of this endeavor, Ben Ali even went so far as proposing to the UN that '2010 be proclaimed as the International Year of Youth' and that 'a world youth congress be held [that year] under the aegis of the United Nations' – an initiative adopted by the General Assembly in its 64th session. These efforts at outreach were being undertaken as young Tunisians were showing increasing signs of disaffection from various official political institutions, as attendance at cultural and youth centers under the auspices of the Ministry of Cultural Affairs (whose meager budget never reached the 1% required by UNESCO) confirmed. Importantly, this alienation was not solely a manifestation of antipathy towards the Ben Ali regime; even after the revolution, in 2014, the number of young people attending youth centers did not exceed 71,627 (47,106 boys and 24,521 girls) (Statistiques Tunisie 2013-2014). Indeed, official statistics show that attendance at the youth venues known as 'Youth Houses' (*Maisons des Jeunes*) and 'Culture Houses' (*Maisons de Culture*) was in fact much lower.

Yet in the backdrop to this apathy towards official institutionalized vectors for youth was a subculture reflecting young people's consternation and revolt through various form of resistance as expressed in daily practices. Football stadiums had on many occasions been the scene of clashes between the forces of law and order and young Ultras not only in the capital but also big cities such as Sousse, Sfax, etc. Likewise, young rappers began recording songs, in groups or solo, which were sharply critical of police practices and government policies, such as rapper Balti's 2005 song 'These (Reclusive) People in Their Corner,' (*Ce gens (reclus) dans leur coin*) which was briefly posted on

37

1 Youtube before it was censored.[1] Such practices of contestation of
2 youth were not relinquished after the fall of Ben Ali but on the contrary
3 were further affirmed and consolidated both during and in the wake of
4 the Tunisian revolution of 2010-2011.

5   These gaps between official vectors for youth participation and
6 alternative forms of resistance and engagement are puzzling precisely
7 because they do not fit a neat dichotomy of the pre- and the post-Ben
8 Ali period. On the contrary, youth political commitment in post-
9 revolutionary Tunisia demonstrates more complex political behaviors
10 that have been adopted in the decade of revolutionary effervescence
11 since 2011. In investigating these behaviors and commitments, I posit
12 that youth political engagement has been reconfigured in a *politics as*
13 *everyday activity*, where political practice ceases to be a distinct pursuit,
14 separate from so-called 'normal' life. Indeed, youth political
15 commitment in Tunisia is being reoriented towards a practice in which
16 subjects (in this case young and individualized subjects), subjectivity,
17 and subjectivization are becoming increasingly influential. Day by day,
18 young people are demonstrating a clearer detachment from the logics
19 that have hitherto presided over the practices of political actors in
20 Tunisia, even in the first post-revolutionary period (until the end of
21 2014).

22   Starting from young people's experience of political engagement
23 and practice as active subjects, the research is based both on semi-
24 structured interviews as well as participant observation of youth in their
25 most natural living and activity environment. I have privileged an
26 epistemological stance that gives primary attention to actors'
27 statements and their most personal expressions of their worldview.
28 Based on this work, I argue that among youth in post-revolutionary
29 Tunisia, subjectivization is the mode by which politics is appropriated,
30 and subjectivity is both their yardstick for interpreting politics and their
31 standpoint/positioning within the political sphere.

32   ## Rethinking Tunisian Youth Political Engagement

33   In this text, I use the term 'youth' not as a generational category or
34 a social category - the social affiliations of the young people I am

---

[1] In the song, he denounced a corrupt police force and judiciary ready to commit all sorts of abuses against people 'without defense or means.' This was the case with several other tracks as well. See Nouri (2012) for more.

1 interested in are so similar that this variable ceases to be relevant - but
2 rather as a way of living the world. In my sense, in a political context,
3 'youth' is above all a way of (un)doing the world. These young people
4 rework and reformulate the relationship that they have with politics
5 and the political world through their political commitment. Concepts
6 and ideas – such as the State, civil society, and governance – are
7 reviewed and redefined. In its relationship with politics and political
8 action, the notion of youth takes on a prefigurative meaning.

9 Above all, this means that we cannot speak of young people as a
10 monolithic entity; rather, from the theoretical-conceptual perspective
11 of this paper, youth is understood as a configuration of practices. The
12 Tunisian post-revolutionary political context means that these practices
13 are generally dissident in their relationship to official, classical, and
14 dominant practices. This dissent, moreover, is intended to be
15 noticeable in the very nature of the activities themselves: their forms,
16 places, and temporalities. Importantly, though, this dissent also
17 presupposes a different way of governing. Indeed, young people insist
18 that their participation should be as broad and free as possible, without
19 hindrance of gender, socio-professional category, or geographical
20 origin. In this way, social justice is a central element in the dissent of
21 these youth.

22 Given this, their conception of politics places emphasis on freedom
23 of expression and organization, and favors a just and egalitarian
24 citizenship. This equates to a total rejection of the 'authoritarian
25 political society' in which they spent the first decade of their lives.
26 However, it also prefigures a central revolutionary demand: the logic
27 here is not only to reject the authoritarian political regime, but also to
28 search for the most efficient means to achieve the aspirations of the
29 revolution.

30 All these elements call for a paradigm shift in how we address the
31 issue of the political engagement of Tunisia's youth. Classical analyses
32 are based on supposed disengagement of young people (Mahéo,
33 Dejaeghere, and Stolle 2012), leading to a kind of theoretical impasse
34 that the mobilization of conceptual dualities such as
35 "inclusion/exclusion" cannot solve. My perspective opposes this
36 simple binary. I opt instead for a focus on the possible emergence of a
37 'new' political actor who is the dissident youth in the sense I have just
38 outlined. We are, in fact, far from the revolutionary youth of 2011. For

1   young people in the past few years of post-revolutionary Tunisia,
2   dissidence has not only materialized in acts of civil disobedience or
3   street protests, but has also, and above all, manifested itself in new
4   modes of organization and governance. If there was political
5   disaffection, it was because we were not looking for youth in the right
6   places (traditional political organizations then the ballot box *vs.* new
7   sociability networks then scenes of dissident activism) or at the right
8   times (voting 'appointments' *vs.* created 'events'). This was not their
9   fault. Rather, it is the analysts who wrongly identified this alleged
10   disengagement. Reports by observer missions, especially European
11   ones, have been full of formulations such as 'the data from the electoral
12   register show that young people and women are under-represented:
13   young people aged 18 to 21, who make up around 10% of the
14   population of voting age, but less than 5% of those registered…' Such
15   statistics are used in scientific articles as field data to assess political
16   engagement (Gobe and Chouikha 2015). Yet the official political scene,
17   with its representative and partisan political structures, has long ceased
18   to be the topos of political practice for young people.

19   The erroneous analyses have also overshadowed the other central
20   element of youth politics in Tunisia, namely communication via
21   increasingly new and changing technologies. Unlike Arab youth from
22   the Mashrek and Gulf countries, who are better versed in the
23   blogosphere of Twitter, young Tunisians, like their Algerian and
24   Moroccan neighbors, are more likely to use Facebook (Lecomte 2011).
25   The remarkable drop in the price of mobile devices and the increasing
26   ease of connecting to the internet (via 4G) only amplify the interest in
27   social networks. The influence that social media has on all forms of
28   youth sociability and participation in collective activities and social life
29   in general cannot be overlooked. It must be stressed here that
30   information and communication technologies (ICTs) play not only a
31   technical or instrumental role in facilitating access to information and
32   the dissemination of ideas, but also a mediating role in allowing greater
33   personal and individualized appropriation of politics (Tourrilhes 2008).

34   It is from this perspective that I question the 'old' concept of
35   'participation.' The latter was used in analyses to evoke the different
36   strategies of integration and inclusion, calling for youth participation,
37   such as external mobilization strategies that invited young people to
38   'feature' somewhere on an official political stage as described above,

1   without changing the operational mechanisms. This participation,
2   when it took place, resulted in a caricature of political commitment: it
3   did nothing to change youth's subaltern status, maintained by non-
4   youths against young people's desire to emancipate their actions and
5   liberate their discourse. Indeed, only very few young people managed
6   to escape this schema of subalternity and become successful actors
7   themselves, and even then only as a few drops through the sieves of
8   the establishment's system of elite reproduction.

9   To reach out to this new youth, we need a paradigm shift. The shape
10   that young people's political action takes based on their own demands
11   should be prioritized by observers as well as analysts: exercising their
12   right to speak as actors who are fully present and fully responsible for
13   their visions and actions, in a world that they have every right to want
14   to unmake and remake, and to be recognized as having rights. As well
15   as analyzing the collective action of the different groups and associated
16   demands, it is therefore judicious to start with a better understanding
17   of these actions themselves. It is imperative to consider them as
18   personal appropriations, i.e. acts of subjectivization, through
19   personalized conceptions and representations that are reflected in a
20   committed practice demonstrating performed meanings.

21   To this point, the different performances and achievements of
22   young people's agency must be at the heart of analyses. My analysis is
23   not meant to be factual but to be fully comprehensive of the know-
24   how brought to bear in the various political actions of young people. I
25   want to identify attempts to produce not only a new world but a
26   specific knowledge of this real world through different representations,
27   conceptions, and interpretive schemes. There are observable and
28   recognizable communities of practice (Wenger 1998) that are fully alive
29   and implementing different kinds of knowledge by all means possible,
30   of which the teleology of practices is the most perfect symbiosis – both
31   among community members and between the community and its living
32   environment, its *mondo*.[2]

33   Methodologically, this same world – which is the 'framework of life'
34   and 'framework for life' of the youth community, its *hic et nunc* – is the
35   socio-historical framework of this research, allowing us to see the
36   evolution of young people in situ. The framework is an embodiment

---

[2] This Italian term is often used by young people with an Arabized pronunciation that lengthens it and gives it a certain musicality.

1   of prefiguration, so much so that the performing practice that evolves
2   there is endowed with meanings originating in the action itself,
3   however dissident it may be. The different autonomous zones of
4   dissident action (Bey 1991) that young people manage to create within
5   these frameworks have two dimensions, spatial-temporal and political-
6   cultural.

7   Spatially, young people's living environments are places of new
8   sociability: neighborhoods, their surroundings, their borders and
9   boundaries, cafés and other places of conviviality and creativity, streets
10   and other theatres for events, city squares, especially if they are
11   conducive to sit-ins, adjacent to local and/or regional authorities, more
12   or less improvised stage spaces for artistic performances and shows,
13   especially in the Street Art style, walls transformed into supports for
14   graffiti, etc. Culturally, the practice is wholly political. Not only because
15   it allows expression, but also, and above all, because it better cements
16   this community of practice, which is always capable and ready to
17   reconfigure/metamorphose itself into a community of taste within the
18   space of an 'event.' Through their practices, which are constantly being
19   made and unmade, young people transform the 'frameworks of life'
20   that surround them into a 'framework for life,' and thus succeed in
21   transforming the world. As a result of their practices, the street is no
22   longer a street, and the square is no longer a square. They instead
23   become a hotbed of dissent. It is through these communities'
24   interventions in the life of the city, reconfiguring spaces and their
25   functions, that they practice and live politics.

26   It is in this sense that the political behavior of Tunisian youth
27   activists in the context of post-revolutionary political effervescence can
28   be understood as politics as everyday activity. Put another way, political
29   practice ceases to take place as a distinct activity at a distributed place
30   and time, an activity that is removed from the normal course of life,
31   and is instead inserted into in a more organic way. Further, I believe it
32   safe to assume that, further downstream, the flipside of politics as an
33   everyday activity will be a politicization of the everyday.

34   Methodological Considerations

35   The research is based on qualitative field work, guided by young
36   people's political practices themselves. The sample is based on a
37   regional division of the country: large urban centers where youth

1   political behavior is influenced by variables such as the demographic
2   concentration of young people (students or others) and the presence
3   of politically-oriented associations and organizations with recruitment
4   capacity; and smaller cities (which, it should be remembered, were the
5   focus of the first actions of the revolution of 17 December 2010 – 14
6   January 2011) whose reduced concentration of youth and associational
7   life impacts the capacity of young people to concretize their political
8   commitment. This difference between 'arenas' and 'forms' of youth
9   political engagement can give rise to a 'concomitant variation:' the
10 larger the arena, the more diverse the forms, and vice versa. Indeed, in
11 some cases, this variation can be promoted to a 'distinction' in the
12 sociological sense. To analyze the types of youth political commitment
13 based on the above-mentioned elements, I have tried to bring together
14 sociological variables that are traditionally observed in any sampling,
15 within a contextualization that has taken the concomitant variations
16 between arenas and forms into consideration.

17   Semi-structured interviews were carried out in 2017-2018 with 50
18 activists (two-thirds men and one-third women), representing different
19 governorates and various institutional affiliations.[3] While the sample
20 represents a mixture of students or those who have already graduated,
21 it does not take into account socio-professional category, given that
22 most in the sample belong to the category of 'unemployed graduates'
23 and are thus somewhat outside the economy, thereby reducing the
24 importance of this variable in the production of the social practices
25 observed. Interviews focused on biographical questions related to the
26 activist's curriculum, experience, and representations (i.e. how they
27 represent their action, policy(ies), relations with youth and non-youth
28 actors in the political sphere, etc.). In addition, other themes raised
29 during the interviews were the values of young people, their social
30 ideals (social justice, freedoms, economic and social rights, evaluation
31 of trade union activism in the field, etc.). Focus groups were also
32 included in the research design, which took the shape of informal
33 dialogues and discussions. Finally, the research benefited from
34 observations, interviews, and discussions carried out during the

---

[3] This includes sit-in committees; street poets; Jil Jadid (youth political organization); neighborhood
networks; rapporteurs and graffiti men; anti-pollution initiatives; citizen journalists; cultural cafés;
student movements; artistic producers; and the Manish Msameh campaign against the so-called
administrative reconciliation law initiated by former President Beji Caid Essebsi. See Ben Said (2017)
for more.

1   Summer Schools of various Tunisian social movements in 2016-2018.[4]
2   I was able to then complete, clarify, and correct the evidence I had
3   collected during the first half of 2019. Some of the data supporting the
4   analyses in this text are based on observations made during the 2018
5   and 2019 elections: the municipal elections of May 2018, the two
6   rounds of the 2019 presidential elections (15 September and 13
7   October respectively) and the legislative elections of 06 October 2019.
8   Finally, the process of evidence gathering also benefitted from
9   materials gathered on various websites and Facebook groups.

10   ## The Logics of Youth Political Engagement

11   In the four to five years preceding the elections of autumn 2019, the
12   political situation in Tunisia was characterized by a withdrawal of
13   young activists from the official political scene (Kchouk and Ben
14   Rhouma 2019). This was especially true once the revolutionary
15   momentum began to peter out and the process known as 'democratic
16   transition' was announced, marked by the meeting of political leaders
17   Beji Caid Essebsi (who would go on to become president from 2014-
18   2019) and Rached Ghannouchi (the historical leader of the Islamist
19   party Ennahdha and current parliament speaker) in the summer of
20   2013. The ensuing political agreement accelerated the disengagement
21   of young people from an official political scene that is increasingly
22   condensed because of its highly partisan, representative, and traditional
23   nature. The political assassinations of Chokri Belaid (6 February 2013)
24   and Mohamed Brahmi (25 July 2013) had already raised doubts and
25   fears among young people, who were less and less convinced by a
26   democratic transition taking place via concessions to figures from the
27   former regime.

28   Seen from below, and especially from the perspective of young
29   people in the working-class neighborhoods of large urban centers and
30   other hubs of the protest movement, the official political scene is
31   hardly hospitable. Several testimonies recount experiences that young

---

[4] Various Tunisian social movements were able to hold their First Summer University (from 23-25 September 2016) and a First Congress (24-26 March 2017). The Second Summer University of Social Movements was held (8-10 September 2018) before the Second Congress was organized (30 March - 01 April 2018). The National Coordination of Social Movements (CNMST) was created at the end of the first Summer University. All these events were organized by the National Coordination with the material and organizational assistance of the Tunisian Forum of Economic and Social Rights (FTDES). Most interviews and focus groups took place in 2017 and 2018 on the fringes of events organized by CNMST and FTDES.

1 people can only relate with bitterness. They use disconcerted,
2 disappointed, and even angry expressions, sometimes with black
3 humor, to illustrate their experiences within both associations and
4 political parties. They speak of the lack of freedom, the narrow
5 perimeters for their own initiatives, whether as an individual or a group,
6 family and/or regional forms of nepotism, the phenomenon of
7 stardom that erodes camaraderie, excessive centralism, the lack of
8 participation in decision-making processes, etc. And for girls and
9 women, all of the above was exacerbated by sexism and misogyny, even
10 in left-wing organizations.

11 In such situations, and compared to what they had expected and
12 their representation(s) of politics, youth found themselves at odds with
13 the atmosphere that prevails in organized political groupings. Their
14 disappointing and even painful experiences have only convinced them
15 all the more of the need to reject partisan and ideologically determined
16 commitment. They noticeably avoid using terms that could refer to
17 such allegiance. In the course of such experimentation with official and
18 institutionalized engagement, political affiliations markedly loosened.
19 While some in the CNMST are partisan, others are non-affiliated, and
20 'formerly party-affiliated' activists. And even though the party
21 affiliations (whether past or still in force, weak or not, formal or
22 informal) are for the most part on the political left, they are nonetheless
23 diversified. In campaigning, party activists are called upon to 'behave'
24 as 'individually committed comrades.' This diminution of partisan
25 belonging allowed campaigns such as Manish Msameh to bring
26 together friends, classmates, fellow students, neighbors, and old
27 acquaintances, offering for some the space for real reunion. As a case
28 in point, during the struggles, demonstrations, sit-ins,
29 commemorations, and other instances of collective action, the term
30 'comrade,' formerly reserved for those sharing partisan affiliation,
31 came to be used in a much more open way.

32 The personal stories about cooptation and mobilization within
33 parties or organizations (followed or not by demobilization) stuck to a
34 similar path. The young activists explained that they not only feel
35 removed from political parties, but also from trade unions and
36 traditional NGOs. As one youth activist stated in an interview: 'I have
37 always known that civil society organizations and associations are
38 feudally ruled by the RCD [Rassemblement Constitutionnel

1　Démocratique, a defunct party presided over by Ben Ali and dissolved
2　by a court ruling in March 2011.]'. Instead, interviewees explain how
3　they organized themselves into real or virtual networks and rhizomes.
4　They have invested the virtual world and in particular via Facebook.
5　Their new structures are governed horizontally. Members are not
6　known to have personal interests to defend within them. They belong
7　to the urban and generally highly educated middle classes, which are
8　capable of supporting young people for longer or shorter periods of
9　unemployment, thus enabling them to be always present without
10　transforming their commitment into activist professionalism, as would
11　be the case within NGOs, especially those with good relations with
12　European donors. The reasons underlying these new forms of youth
13　political resistance were already tangible in 2008 (Chouikha and Gobe
14　2009).

15　　In terms of political discourse and symbols, young people's
16　rejection of official political jargon and the 'politically correct' is an
17　innovation in content. There is a certain perception of generational
18　conflict among them: they claim different political values from their
19　elders. Whereas the previous generation based itself on identity and
20　ideology, the new generation emphasizes concepts of the good life for
21　everyone, an 'organic' way of life on all fronts. This translates into a
22　desire to implement a truly revolutionary process of social
23　transformation that goes beyond simple democratic transition. Young
24　people told me that they were interested in socio-economic issues,
25　social justice, and equity between regions. They told me about their
26　fatigue, their disgust with politics as it is played out on the official stage,
27　and their disdain for this never-ending 'transition,' which the country
28　navigates purely by sight and which results in the total absence of real
29　change.

30　　Youth political discourse is subjective, with strong symbolic
31　connotations. There are elements here that can be translated into the
32　sense of a culturing (Diop and Pedrazzini 2000)[5] of political practices.
33　These are no longer purely political in the sense that the older
34　generation of activists used to stage them. Rap, graffiti, slam, and other
35　forms of street art have played a major role in this phenomenon of
36　culturing. Within youth movements and initiatives, there is also a

---

[5] In the sense that Moussa Diop and Yves Pedrazzini develop in their study on Latin America, Europe and Africa (Diop and Pedrazzini 2000).

1 tendency towards symbolic action in a way that creates new forms of
2 sociability. Manish Msameh's sit-ins and demonstrations, for example,
3 feature clowns, Ultras-style flares, and a drummer. In the case of the
4 latter, his trajectory exemplifies this tendency: an agricultural engineer
5 by training who has never worked in his field, and who left paid
6 employment with an NGO after a few months, he borrowed the drum
7 from an Ultra friend and explained that his drumming helped to better
8 'musicalize' the chanting of slogans. The flares turn the event into a
9 real spectacle that appeals to young people who are used to such scenes
10 from the stands of football stadiums.

11   Among their slogans is one that expresses young people's disdain
12 for the political regime, which they feel has been eroded and afflicted
13 with necrosis. Using the name of a farm that was depicted in a
14 children's soap opera produced and broadcast on the Tunisian national
15 television channel in 1995-1996, they make reference to this common
16 cultural 'heritage' to stylize criticism of the post-revolutionary Tunisian
17 state as non-revolutionary, eaten away as it is by elements of the past
18 which it incorporates anew.

19   This tinkering with the term 'politics' is a manifestation of what I
20 call the 'hybridization of politics.' I have cited elements of this in terms
21 of design, representation, and practice. The effect of culturing and
22 hybridization, as characteristics of youth political practices and
23 conceptions, is so strong that we can speak of the 'youthfulness' of
24 politics in post-revolutionary Tunisia. Year by year, the demands of
25 Tunisia's youth, which it has chanted from the first days of the
26 revolution, have gained ground, support, and supporters so as to
27 become the demands of society as a whole. It is true that in '2014,
28 almost a third of the population (32.1%) was under the age of 20 and
29 half (49.3%) under the age of 30.' (Statistiques Tunisie 2017, 11).
30 However, this demographic dimension cannot fully explain the
31 phenomenon of youthfulness. Youth political propaganda has reached
32 all strata of society. Even those who take a negative view of this
33 upheaval in the State-society relationship to the benefit of the latter are
34 not exempt from it. A possible sociology of aspirations might argue
35 that blocking young people's aspirations in fact blocks the whole logic
36 of social and upward mobility, and is thus the strongest expression of
37 the difficulty of being young (Melliti, Mahfoudh-Draoui, Ben Amor,
38 and Ben Fredj 2008) in a society that itself struggles to ensure a social

1   transition towards a more just society. Such analyses and others in the
2   same vein, dating from well before the revolution, have shown (despite
3   the authors' tendency to stress the different kinds of identity crises
4   experienced by young Tunisians) that these difficulties begin in
5   adolescence (Melliti and Mahfoudh-Draoui 2006).

6   The territorialization of movements and demands has meant that all
7   major cities have been affected by this youth political propaganda. But
8   the political commitment of young people outside the big cities is also
9   remarkable. The hotbeds of revolutionary tension are to be found in
10   the west and south of the country. Territorialization furthermore also
11   is manifested at the sectoral level. Primary and secondary school
12   teachers, high school students and pupils, young doctors and
13   unemployed graduates have relayed responsibility for the social
14   struggle between themselves over the last five years. The contagion
15   effects of this territorialization, which is thus as much spatial as
16   sectoral, are easily felt. The older sections of the population are won
17   over to the cause and support the claims and aspirations of the young.

18   The following diagram summarizes my findings:

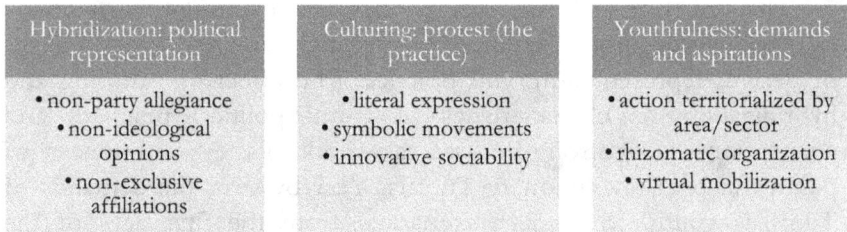

Hybridization: political representation	Culturing: protest (the practice)	Youthfulness: demands and aspirations
• non-party allegiance • non-ideological opinions • non-exclusive affiliations	• literal expression • symbolic movements • innovative sociability	• action territorialized by area/sector • rhizomatic organization • virtual mobilization

19

Politics as Everyday Activity

21   One aspect of the hybridization of young Tunisians' political
22   engagement in post-revolutionary Tunisia is the fact that there are
23   young people who are not reluctant to engage with the 'traditional
24   political sector.' Some youth sectors do not do so; others do so only
25   within civil society associations; and yet others only if it is in line with
26   their norms and modes of engagement. In terms of the depth and
27   importance of this coordination, some youth sectors are more involved
28   than others and sometimes find themselves having to 'justify' such
29   tactics. Such differing positions reveal differences in tactics in the sense
30   of seeking solutions to practical problems. The interviews revealed that

1 young Tunisian activists have indeed repeatedly been faced with
2 operational problems: lack of premises, lack of funding, poor control
3 of relations with traditional NGOs, ambiguous relations with donors,
4 the omnipresence of the security concerns in their conflicts with law
5 enforcement and public authorities in general, a cyclical
6 narrowing/reopening of public space, restrictions on freedom of
7 assembly and association, etc. Several campaigns have been mounted
8 to denounce 'the criminalization of social movements.' Young activists
9 also have needs in terms of media strategies that are difficult to address.
10 The various attempts to lift the media blockade around youth activism
11 and practices are vital. Such tactics represent resistance to asphyxiation
12 and silent death; they are tactics to preserve life in its material sense.
13 Yet, they are also tactics in the sense of preserving social existence.
14 Despite the difficulties I have listed, young Tunisian activists in post-
15 revolutionary Tunisia show a very high capacity for negotiation.
16 Generally, the latter is done collectively, based on a division of labor
17 and the strengthening of links with organized local communities.
18 Through such means and other resources, sit-ins were able to last for
19 months, and campaigns were able to revive when they were thought
20 dead. By providing tactical room for maneuver, these resources enable
21 young people to keep the movements autonomous to a certain extent.
22 This jealously guarded autonomy is manifested, for example, in the
23 ability of young people to resist repeated attempts at cooptation by the
24 political parties.

25   The political practices of young people in medium-sized towns in
26 the country's center-west and south-east are the most edifying
27 examples of this logic of preserving social existence. The municipal
28 elections of 06 May 2018 highlighted the capacities of young
29 independent people, who were able to improvise candidate lists, build
30 coalitions, and tailor 'electoral' groups across the country. Here, too,
31 the logics of hybridization and territorialization worked well. Many
32 independent and youth-dominated lists achieved convincing results,
33 surpassing the political parties. Political competition with 'adversaries'
34 of the traditional political scene is easier for young people in such areas,
35 as they have the means and resources necessary. All the political activity
36 they had carried out in the first weeks of the revolution enabled them
37 to take advantage of a political 'career,' a 'credit' that can be proudly
38 mobilized.

1   Tactics to preserve social existence thus give rise to practices that
2   seek political recognition. The main argument against the old political
3   elite mobilized by these 'outsiders' who strive to be 'insiders' is that the
4   elite (regardless of political affiliation) is unable to make things happen
5   and bring about change. The logic that prevails here is that of
6   rebalancing the local political spheres and redistributing power and
7   influence within them. This logic is achieved through almost daily
8   negotiations with the authorities, collaboration agreements with local
9   organizations and communities, and the deployment of safeguards to
10   protect institutional autonomy. The specific methods used in putting
11   this logic into practice vary greatly from one region to another, but are
12   in operation throughout the country. In some cases they give rise to
13   the development of real 'strategies' that may or may not be shared. For
14   the dissemination of these practices, activists favor Facebook, using
15   information pages and calls for mobilization, closed discussion groups,
16   etc., which makes them relatively reproducible examples.

17   Youth groups no longer take the shape of political parties, political
18   organizations, or even civil society organizations, NGOs or others. The
19   two strategic characteristics of the new forms of youth organization are
20   flexibility and horizontality. Like social networks, they too embody the
21   twin tactics of preserving material life and social existence. The
22   development of networks does not mean an absence of centers and
23   peripheries within them. However, these positions are interchangeable.
24   The horizontal, democratic, and participatory aspects of action by these
25   communities reinforce this interchangeability. They are more durable
26   than any other possible form of organization. Because they are flexible,
27   their strength is made out of their weakness; it is indeed built into their
28   weakness.

29   They are directly solvent in daily life, not only in that their members
30   but of the entire surrounding community. These networks can go on
31   standby, relax, replenish, and dilute themselves. A network is
32   maintained on an almost daily basis through activities that traditionally
33   are not considered political because they do not directly and openly
34   target political power. In practice, these structures vary in activity over
35   times, depending on the 'seriousness' of situations and the acuity of
36   events. The degree of commitment of their 'members' can also
37   fluctuate from one activist to another, depending on the impact on
38   their availability of family, education, and work. A network activist for

1   a specific cause can be put on standby for weeks or even months. The
2   ties that unite its members are not affected, because a specific political
3   action can leave room for an artistic practice considered to be perfectly
4   in line with it, and where 'recruitment' is carried for possible future
5   campaigns.

6   From the point of view of territorialization, the political campaigns
7   in which the young members of these movements are involved are
8   mainly urban, although some quasi-rural movements have also
9   emerged, often in small and medium-sized towns such as Kasserine,
10   Sidi Bouzid, Menzel Bouzayene, Regueb, etc. Here, family and
11   community relations are reworked and relabeled relations of mutual
12   political commitment. It is true that these reworked and relabeled
13   relationships are contractual and of short duration, but they often open
14   up new avenues of renewable solidarity. This renewal does not
15   necessarily take place in politics or through politics. It is the irresolvable
16   issue of social justice that makes these renewals of solidarity possible
17   and their necessity constantly felt, requested, sought, and wanted.
18   Public policies and their highly negative overall outcomes only prove
19   these young people right.

20   The latest manifestation of the hybridization of politics among
21   young Tunisian activists is their role in the election of Kais Saied to the
22   presidency of the republic. Several reports have referred to Saied's
23   victory as the victory of youth. He was their candidate. This does not
24   mean that all sectors of young people rallied to him. On this very issue,
25   there is disagreement among my interlocutors. However, it should be
26   noted that while the first round of the 2019 presidential election was
27   shunned by 55% of voters (Verdier 2019), *Jeune Afrique* reported that,
28   for the final battle, 'several private Facebook groups have campaigned
29   for the constitutionalist (Saied) in recent weeks, under the name "Kais
30   Saied President of the Republic" for example, which alone has nearly
31   100,000 members, "Change the Future," "Youth of the Future," "Sahel
32   Group," or "Kais Saied for the Constituent Assembly"' (Lafrance
33   2019). This ultimate aspect of the hybridization of youth political
34   commitment in post-revolutionary Tunisia deserves a more detailed
35   analysis that is beyond the scope of this paper. However, it should be
36   noted that data provided by the Independent High Electoral Body
37   (ISIE) show a voter mobilization that merits further investigation:
38   'contrary to all calculations and forecasts [...] it is young people aged

1 18 to 25 […] who constitute the overwhelming majority of new voters,
2 namely 70% or 880,000, with less than one week to go before the end
3 of the voter registration period' (Dermech 2019). This was a genuine
4 investment by the young people who seem to have once again to
5 changed tactics.

Conclusion

7 Political commitment by Tunisian youth in post-revolutionary
8 Tunisia has had its own revolution. It occurred rather late compared to
9 the 2010-2011 Revolution, namely a few years later. In the meantime,
10 the gap that separated Tunisia's youth from its former political elite was
11 widening and becoming more pronounced. This chasm was expressed
12 through various forms of dissidence. The political commitment of
13 young Tunisians in post-revolutionary Tunisia has mainly revolved
14 around the quest for social justice. Along the way, their rejection of the
15 authoritarian social and political order has been strengthened through
16 subjective relationships with politics and the political scene. The quest
17 for social justice, often transformed into tactics for the preservation of
18 material life, has faithfully translated the demands and aspirations of a
19 youth increasingly present in politics without necessarily being
20 apparent on the official political stage. To them, that stage seems more
21 and more traditional, defined by party politics, the logic of electoral
22 representation, and thus (s)elective.

23 Among young people, politics is no longer the subject of a quasi-
24 professional commitment. It is becoming more cultural, symbolic,
25 hybrid, and diversified both by area and by sector. By the same token,
26 it is losing its specificity as well as its transcendentality. By combining
27 hybridization, culturing, and youthfulness, youth political practices
28 create politics as an everyday activity. The difference between the
29 political sphere and the 'non-political' sphere is eliminated. Which in
30 turn opens the door for future investigation to explore whether this
31 politics as everyday activity necessarily leads to the politicization of the
32 everyday.

References

34 Ben Said, Esma. 2017. "Tunisie: Adoption de la loi sur la réconciliation
35   administrative." Accessed September 19, 2020. https://www.aa.com.tr/
36   fr/afrique/tunisie-adoption-de-la-loi-sur-la-r%C3%A9conciliation-

1   administrative/909642

2   Bey, Hakim. 2011. The Temporary Autonomous Zone: Ontological Anarchy,
3   Political Terrorism. Brooklyn, New York: Autonomedia.

4   Chouikha, Larbi and Éric Gobe. 2009. "La Tunisie entre la 'révolte du bassin
5   minier de Gafsa' et l'échéance électorale de 2009." L'Année du Maghreb 5.
6   Accessed July 24, 2020. http://journals.openedition.org/anneemaghreb/
7   623

8   Dermech, Abdelkrim. 2019. "Isie - enregistrement des électeurs : Les jeunes
9   reviennent en force." *La Presse*, May 17, 2019.

10   Diop, Moussa and Yves Pedrazzini. 2000. "La lutte et la boxe au service de la
11   paix : A Dakar, des gangs s'organisent contre la violence urbaine." In *La*
12   *violence urbaine vue des quartiers de Dakar : Recherche populaire et autoévaluation*
13   *dans trois quartiers de la capitale sénégalaise*, edited by Moussa Diop, 67-70.
14   Paris : Editions Charles Léopold Mayer.

15   Gobe, Éric and Larbi Chouikha. 2015. "La Tunisie de la Constitution aux
16   élections : La fin de la transition politique ?" L'Année du Maghreb 13.
17   Accessed July 24, 2020. http://journals.openedition.org/anneemaghreb/
18   2602

19   Kchouk, Bilel and Amel Ben Rhouma. (2019). "Gouvernance politique,
20   diversité du genre et transition démocratique : leçons tunisiennes."
21   Maghreb-Machrek 2(240): 93-120.

22   Lafrance, Camille. 2019. "Présidentielle en Tunisie : enquête sur les réseaux
23   qui ont porté Kaïs Saïed au second tour." *Jeune Afrique*, November 12,
24   2019.

25   Lecomte, Romain. 2011. " Révolution tunisienne et Internet : le rôle des
26   médias sociaux " L'Année du Maghreb 7. Accessed July 24, 2020.
27   http://journals.openedition.org/anneemaghreb/1288;

28   Mahéo, Valérie-Anne, Dejaeghere, Yves and Dietlind Stolle. 2012. "La non-
29   participation politique des jeunes: Une étude des barrières temporaires et
30   permanentes de l'engagement." *Canadian Journal of Political Science / Revue*
31   *canadienne de science politique* 45(2): 405-425.

32   Melliti, Imed, Mahfoudh-Draoui, Dorra, Ben Amor, Ridha and Slaheddine
33   Ben Fredj. 2008. *Jeunes, dynamiques identitaires et frontières culturelles* Tunis:
34   UNICEF.

35   Melliti, Imed and Dorra Draoui-Mahfoudh. 2006. *De la difficulté de grandir. Pour*
36   *une sociologie de l'adolescence en Tunisie*. Tunis: Centre de Publication
37   Universitaire.

38   Nouri, Gana. 2012. "Rap and Revolt in the Arab World." *Social Text* 30 (4):
39   25–53.

40   Statistiques Tunisie. 2017. "Recensement général de la population. Jeunesse
41   et vieillesse à travers le RGPH 2014." Accessed September 18, 2020.
42   http://www.ins.tn/sites/default/files/publication/pdf/Livret-Jeunesse-
43   vieillesse.pdf

Statistiques Tunisie. 2013-2014. "Tunisie en Chiffres." Accessed September 19, 2020. http://www.ins.tn/sites/default/files/publication/pdf/tec-newform-51-web%20%281%29.pdf

Tourrilhes, Catherine. 2008. "Mediation, Social Innovation or New Mode of Regulation? Vers des espaces tiers de socialisation" *Pensée plurielle* 2(18): 109-120.

Verdier, Marie. 2019. "En Tunisie, les jeunes plébiscitent le « révolutionnaire-conservateur » Kais Saied." La Croix, September 16, 2019.

Wenger, Etienne. 1998. *Communities of Practice: Learning, Meaning and Identity.* Cambridge: Cambridge University Press.

THE IMAGINED COMMUNITY OF LEBANESE YOUTH ACTIVISTS: POLITICAL RESISTANCE BY OTHER MEANS?

Khaled Nasser

The last decade of Lebanese youth activism shows a trajectory that seems somewhat incongruous with that of regional neighbors. Having largely sat out the broader revolutionary movements in 2011, youth activism seemed to join the Arab Spring in 2015 with the YouStink movement, which saw grievances move from issue-based claims around the garbage crisis to much broader calls for wide-ranging reform of the sectarian political system. While this movement failed to produce regime change, it none the less laid the foundations for the emergence of new generation political forces that challenged outright sectarian political party logic. Yet after some initial electoral success, these new efforts also seemed to fade away. Then in October 2019, revolutionary mobilization arrived in earnest, calling for an overhaul of the entire political class under the collective banner "All Means All," only to dissipate under the crushing weight of Covid-19. In parallel to these protest waves and various manifestations of direct political contestation has been a plethora of new youth initiatives in various forms of public service within the country's diverse civil society sector, which aim to either work with the State or indeed fill in gaps where the State is absent.

While the provision of public services and direct political activism calling for systemic change do not seem to go hand-in-hand, investigation into youth activists across these different fields of social and political engagement reveals a shared political subjectivity and collective self-conceptualization. In assessing Lebanese youth civic and political activism from the perspective of the youth themselves, placing their own subjectivity centrally in the analytical framework, this paper reveals an imagined community, the Civil Society, in which youth activists conceive of themselves as connected through a shared positionality in the broader sectors of civil society and the traditional political arena, but also linked in joint enterprise: that of political

1   resistance. Using practice theory (Adler and Pouliot 2011) and
2   Anderson's imagined community framework (1991), the study
3   evaluates how youth civic and political activism positions itself in the
4   largely static sectarian political environment. Based on 25 semi-
5   structured interviews and three focus group discussions with youth
6   activists across a variety of service provision and political activism
7   organizations and initiatives carried out from September 2017 –
8   January 2018, as well as a policy dialogue with new generation political
9   forces in the aftermath of their failed electoral bids in 2018, the study
10 offers critical insight into how Lebanese youth conceive of themselves
11 as an activist community. The study reveals that, despite a converging
12 understanding of their action as a form of political resistance, the
13 means by which this is to be achieved and the actual impact on the
14 political system produce diverging relationships with the State and
15 competing tension of system maintenance/system change. The study
16 also reveals how their own self-conceptualization as a community apart
17 has at times led to isolation and an inability to connect with purported
18 constituents. This study thus sheds critical light on the meanings and
19 practices of Lebanese youth civic and political activism in the in-
20 between years after the 2011 Arab Spring and before October 2019
21 Revolution, and allows for a deeper understanding of the connections
22 between the different forms and waves of activism but also the
23 difficulties in building from one iteration to the next.

24

Under-Theorizing Lebanese Youth Activism

26   While the study of Lebanese civil society and its evolution has
27 received important theoretical attention in the literature, the study of
28 youth political activism and various forms of youth civil society
29 participation has received much less conceptual investigation. As with
30 many other studies of Arab youth political activism, especially in the
31 immediate wake of 2011 (see for example Allagui and Kuebler 2011;
32 Cavatorta 2012), the Lebanese case has been studied through the
33 vector of resources, focusing on new forums and media for youth to
34 express grievances and how these have allowed youth voices to invest
35 the public sphere. Likewise, the literature has focused to a degree on
36 the ephemeral nature of this activism, and the inability to form lasting

1   political structures. Such approaches, however, have tended to place
2   emphasis on the form of youth activism rather than rather than its
3   subjective meaning to the activists themselves. As such, this literature
4   does not fully conceptualize what is unique about youth social and
5   political activism in the Lebanese context.

6   Historically, the civil society sector in Lebanon has played a
7   fundamental role providing a wide range of services in public domains,
8   mainly in health, education, social welfare, environment, human rights,
9   politics, civic engagement and advocacy (El-Husseini, Toepler, and
10 Salamon 2004). Studying the development of associations and
11 evolution of civil society writ large, scholars have recognized the close
12 connection of activism to the socio-historic changes in Lebanon
13 (Karam 2006; Haddad 2017), conceptualizing how different forms of
14 activism have emerged in modern times to address changes in State and
15 society. Based on the framework developed by Marchetti and Tocci
16 (2009), Haddad (2017) identifies four major factors that have
17 historically influenced the work of the Lebanese civil society: political
18 context, nature of authority, socio-economic conditions, and level of
19 external interventions.

20   With regards to political context, the level of public services
21 provided by the Lebanese State is directly related to how civil society
22 evolves: the weaker the performance of the State, the more active civil
23 society becomes, and the more focused it is on emergency relief
24 (Marchetti and Tocci 2009). For example, during the Civil War 1975-
25 1990, Lebanese associations collaborated their effort to provide
26 humanitarian and social welfare services (Karam 2006). During the
27 Hezbollah-Israel 2006 war and later the Syrian crisis as of 2011, similar
28 conditions prompted social and charitable organizations and
29 volunteers to assist displaced Lebanese and Syrian refugees
30 respectively.

31   The scope of civil engagement is also influenced by the nature of
32 authority in the country, and in particular, the margin of liberty granted
33 to activists, the level of democracy, and the application of laws
34 (Marchetti and Tocci 2009). As Kingston (2013) observes, civil society
35 in Lebanon acts along a free space between the usually weak
36 government and the dominant sectarian leadership. When the
37 government is strong and the space of freedom to maneuver increases,
38 for instance during the Shehabi reforms in 1958 and during the 2000-

1   2005 period, young activists, who bring fresh perspectives, cooperate
2   with the State in development projects and national reforms (Haddad
3   2017; Karam 2006). When the political elites exercise more authority,
4   however, the space of freedom for civil society decreases. In those
5   conditions, social welfare or "administrative" NGOs tend to increase
6   their cooperation with the political leadership - with successful
7   outcomes - in order to provide the social needs unfulfilled by the weak
8   public services (Clark and Salloukh 2013; Kingston 2013). On the other
9   hand, Lebanese advocacy activists - with less successful impact - tend
10 to apply rather unconventional tactics focusing on human rights issues
11 and social change (Karam 2009). For instance, by the end of the Syrian
12 military presence in Lebanon, young associations were calling for
13 liberties, anti-corruption, and transparency. And after former prime
14 minister Hariri's assassination in 2005, protesters held nationalist
15 messages and called for independence from the Syrian domination
16 (Haddad 2017).

17   The third factor influencing activism in Lebanon is the socio-
18 economic condition of the country (Marchetti and Tocci 2009). During
19 socio-economic hardships, social welfare associations with religious
20 and communal roots, providing basic needs of charity, health, and
21 education, tend to thrive at the expense of national development and
22 advocacy activism. In fact, major Lebanese traditional associations
23 were established by the end of the Ottoman empire and the French
24 mandate to attend in particular to the social difficulties of their religious
25 communities (Haddad 2017). Today, with the increasingly weak
26 economy, the Lebanese elites are maintaining their constituents'
27 dependency and consequently their sectarian-based hegemony through
28 their network of welfare organizations (Kingston 2013).

29   The fourth and last factor relates to the level of interventions of
30 international organizations. The international community, through its
31 funding programs, has helped many local associations gain autonomy
32 in their planning and activities, independently from local authorities
33 (Marchetti and Tocci 2009). Through such funding, international
34 agencies have also empowered some types of local organizations at the
35 expense of others, depending on international agendas as well as local
36 needs. For example, international funders have shifted their focus from
37 supporting developmental programs during and right after the civil war
38 in the 1980s and 1990s to pushing since 2000 for advocacy programs

1   related to human rights, democracy and political engagement, women
2   and youth, and environmental issues (Haddad 2017; Karam 2006).
3   Among them are feminist groups and youth organizations who
4   launched over the past decade several major campaigns focusing on
5   domestic violence, Lebanese nationality rights, and legal marriage age
6   for women.

7   Within these parameters shaping Lebanese civil society in its
8   ensemble, youth have emerged as among the country's chief activist
9   players. The way their activism has been assessed, however, often
10 focuses less on the broader socio-political factors that shape their
11 engagement than the tools of their engagement itself. For example,
12 much attention has been paid to how youth fill the public sphere with
13 their voices and perspectives using a variety of new media tools.
14 Indeed, Lebanese youth have often played a vocal part on the socio-
15 political scene. For instance, the civil war years witnessed a surge of
16 alternative TV and radio stations (Nasr 2011) run by youth, while the
17 Cedar Revolution of 2005 was characterized by the contribution of the
18 youth-led advertising agencies volunteering to create catchy slogans
19 and visuals (Khalil 2017). During the July War in 2006, young activists
20 took advantage of the rise of digital media to counter the international
21 pro-Israel discourse (Fadda-Conrey 2010). Analyzing the "youth-
22 generated" blogging during the 2006 war, Khalil (2017) highlights the
23 creativity, energy, and agency of the youth community at times of crisis.
24 Likewise, activists during the YouStink movements of 2015
25 strategically encouraged and promoted on social media the
26 participation of families with their children in the protests to gain
27 attention and sympathy, emphasizing the impact of the environmental
28 crisis on future generations (Khalil 2017).

29   The research on youth activism has also tended to focus on the
30 personal trajectories of youth activists, revealing for example the
31 importance of personal and family related motivators in influencing
32 engagement levels (Fadda-Conrey 2010). Likewise, a survey on
33 Lebanese civil society by UNDP (El-Amine and Abouchedid 2008)
34 found youth acquire political and human rights values through family
35 socialization - for example, political discussions at home while
36 watching the news. The report also noticed the gendered distribution
37 of activist sectors, with men tending to volunteer in political activism
38 and women favoring other socio-cultural domains. And according to

1   Haugbolle (2007), youth in Lebanon act out of dissonance. Observing
2   behavior that contradicts with principles they learnt at home, they feel
3   compelled to react. They engage in associations or even develop
4   individual initiatives, such as blogging about the atrocities of the 2006
5   war, to help reduce the dissonance they may experience if they remain
6   silent (Haugbolle 2007; Khalil 2012).

7   In this vein youth activism has also received criticism as mere
8   "reactivism," lacking commitment and consistency (Hermez 2011;
9   Sukarieh 2007). Those scholars argue that Lebanese activists are mainly
10   motivated and engaged during emotionally charged events, then by the
11   end of the crisis their efforts fade out and newly formed political
12   networks disintegrate. This was noted in several recent political crises.
13   The political status acquired by the thousands of protesters filling in
14   Martyrs' Square during the 2005 "Independence Revolution" gradually
15   disappeared with the rise of March 8 and March 14 political
16   mainstream coalitions (Karam 2006). Likewise, while more than three
17   hundred bloggers joined the online public sphere in their coverage of
18   the July 2006 Hezbollah-Israel War, many of them reduced their
19   blogging by end of the war (Haugbolle 2007). And during the garbage
20   crisis of 2015, the YouStink youth-based movement, with its
21   unconventional tactics, motivated thousands of Lebanese to take to the
22   streets calling for an immediate solution to the piling waste.
23   Unfortunately, within several years, the movement had virtually
24   disintegrated (Kraidy 2016).

25   In considering youth activism within frames of "reaction/action,"
26   however, these approaches fail to take into consideration both how and
27   why youth activism has evolved over time, or indeed what is particular
28   about youth activism and youth participation in civil society. Yet, by
29   not taking into consideration youth activism from the perspective of
30   the youth activists themselves, it is difficult to understand why
31   movements and youth-led groups seem to quickly assemble and
32   dissemble, and how these movements both fit in with and differ from
33   the broader Lebanese civil society landscape. There is thus a need to
34   place youth activist subjectivity centrally to grasp the links between
35   different waves of mobilization and indeed between different forms of
36   youth civic and political activism.

1   # Youth Activism and the Imagined Community

2   In an attempt to answer what is unique about youth activism in
3   Lebanon, and to move past the more limited framing of
4   "reaction/action," this study seeks to assess Lebanese youth activism
5   within the framework of practice theory (Adler and Pouliot 2011;
6   Reckwitz 2002), placing centrally youth's own conception of their work
7   and how they position themselves vis-à- vis the broader civil society
8   sector as well as the traditional political class. Adler and Pouliot (2011)
9   define practices as "socially meaningful patterns of action, which, in
10   being performed more or less competently, simultaneously embody,
11   act out, and possibly reify background knowledge and discourse in and
12   on the material world" (p. 4). Based on this definition, the authors
13   highlight five key characteristics of practice on which investigation
14   should focus: (1) participants' performance, or the intentional social
15   action or series of actions with specific meaning. Performance is (2)
16   patterned. Those actions tend to be repetitive and follow a sequence.
17   They are socially observable and evaluated based on collectively set (3)
18   standards of competence. Therefore, the practice requires and reflects
19   (4) background knowledge in the form of practical skills, of how to
20   accomplish this performance. Finally, practice is a communal
21   performance, requiring an exchange and use of (5) discourse
22   (communication, language) and material (artifacts, technology).

23   Following this conceptual framework, we seek here to assess youth
24   as a practice of activism rather than an age category, youth as
25   performance rather than as being. More precisely, youth performance
26   is conceived as social engagement, the act of contesting a reality and
27   working to improve it. Scholars have approached the concept of youth
28   activism from very different perspective in terms of activists' age,
29   generational differences, culture, and identity. In this study, we adopt
30   Corsaro's (2005) definition of youth activists as socially engaged
31   performers with self-generated worldviews developed in a dialogic
32   process with the political mainstream.

33   An important consideration of practice is that this social act of
34   doing is situated in relation to a socio-historical context. Youth
35   activism attempts to influence, and is influenced by, existing and
36   changing cultural conditions. How Lebanese youth interpret their
37   engagement with regards to the broader socio-historical context, and
38   more precisely how they situate themselves within the arenas of civil

1   society and the traditional political sphere, thus becomes a primary
2   domain of investigation. More precisely we seek to directly evaluate the
3   extent to which youth activists in the in-between years of post-2011
4   and pre-2019 consider their activism a direct or indirect form of
5   political activism, or rather a form of social service provision as per
6   traditional Lebanese civil society. In this paper, we frame Lebanese
7   youth activists as a community participating in an embodied and
8   discursive performance (what we do), and consequently sharing
9   knowledge related to their particular activity (how we do it), setting
10   group membership guidelines (who is in/out), manifesting a certain
11   social identity (who we are), and giving meaning to their performance.

12   In line with Anderson's imagined community (1991), we attempt to
13   answer the following questions: to what extent do youth activists
14   perceive themselves and consider their input to be part of an
15   "imagined" civil society. How do they distinguish their imagined
16   community from the broader Lebanese civil society sector? And what
17   factors, if any, are heightening this youth activist perception of an
18   imagined community? We posit here that Lebanese youth activists
19   harbor a mindset that differentiates them from the rest of the
20   population and converges them into an imagined community of
21   Lebanese youth activists, known as the Civil Society. We argue in this
22   paper that the Civil Society is an imagined community that is perceived
23   by the youth as a virtual network grouping the different associations
24   and initiatives. The imagined community, moreover, has an ultimate
25   national purpose, that of social change. The identity of this Civil
26   Society is heavily based on the act of doing and finding alternative
27   means to contest the current reality.

28   In order to investigate the nature of this imagined community and
29   the activists' scope of practice, the study used different qualitative
30   methods applied over two evidence-gathering phases, consisting first
31   of 25 in-depth interviews and collected media material (such as social
32   media content, brochures, and other activist and associative materials),
33   and then three focus group discussions with youth activists and civil
34   society   leaders   that   involved   video-elicited   discussion.[1]   For

---

[1] All sessions began with a video-elicited discussion. Participants were asked to watch a three-minute clip about activism in Lebanon. We produced the short video by juxtaposing, over the audio background of the Lebanese anthem, a series of photos collected from the participants during the phase one interviews. The photos depicted Lebanese activists in action, in the field or during group meetings. At the end of the video we asked the following question: "List the ideas, feelings, images,

1 participants' sampling, we attempted to cover a wide range of civil and
2 political activism, focusing specifically on those that either were youth-
3 led or that had significant youth appeal and membership. The
4 performances of the participating organizations or initiatives varied
5 along the following observed categories: 1- political activism, divided
6 between public services, high-power approach (including new political
7 forces such as the Sabaa Party and Beirut Madinati) and civil
8 disobedience, low-power approach (including protest movements such
9 as the YouStink movement), 2- social awareness/educational activism,
10 3- social support/welfare activism, including psychosocial support, 4-
11 right-based/legal activism, and 5- affective activism aimed at spreading
12 positivity and hope. Participants were selected based on a snowballing
13 sampling process, which allowed for the natural contours of the
14 activists' own imagined community to be delineated. Fieldwork was
15 carried out from September 2017 – January 2018, with a follow-up
16 policy dialogue held in November 2018 with new political forces in the
17 aftermath of their failed electoral bids.

Converging Views of Political Resistance, Diverging Relationships to Systemic Change

20 The imagined community of youth activists that was made
21 perceptible through the research can be characterized by numerous
22 shared socioeconomic, linguistic, and cultural markers. As one young
23 activist framed it: "we are a convergence of like-minded people." The
24 activist youth think of themselves as those who have embodied the best
25 of Lebanese values and resisted its worst. The community of activists
26 is rooted in the mid and mid-upper families, living in the cosmopolitan
27 area of Beirut and around it, highly educated in their professional field
28 and in their topic of activism, and well exposed to international political
29 and cultural movements mainly through travel and studying abroad.
30 The English language is commonly used in their oral and written
31 communication, which is reinforced by their frequent coordination or
32 affiliation with international organizations and funders. These youth
33 activists tend to adopt less conservative values than the general public,

---

and people that crossed your mind while watching this video." The video-elicited discussion had several purposes: 1- to serve as an ice-breaker activity for attendees, 2- to prime participants to the topic of activism and social engagement, 3- to help participants perceive their activism from a distance, from a community of practice perspective, beyond the specific scope of their domain, and 4- to assess their overall opinion about the work and impact of the civil society in Lebanon.

1   and have high level of national identification. As one activist put it:
2   "There is a sense of belonging to this country that you love, although
3   it is going through a lot of crisis. Maybe I am selfish, but I want to and
4   it is my right to live in a better country. Also, there is a need to express
5   myself. At one point, I was feeling down, but then you meet people
6   who have the same objectives as you do and you stick with them." As
7   can be seen in this statement, participation in the imagined Civil Society
8   also provides strong feelings of belonging to those participating in the
9   various forms of civic and political activism. This convergence of
10   people that share common values, beliefs, interests, and consequently
11   practices, creates a sense of refuge away from the incongruities of the
12   Lebanese society and empowers activists by providing them the means
13   for self-actualization and social change. As one interviewee said well:
14   "Here, I am able to be away or not in contact with what bothers me in
15   the society. I came from a place where I was very disappointed. The
16   Sabaa (party) helped me fill this gap."

17   While the sampling method deliberately sought to explore youth
18   civil and political activism in a variety of sectors, one of the most
19   interesting findings was the participants shared view of their
20   engagement as an act of political resistance to the prevailing status quo
21   – regardless over whether their activities are linked to politics or not.
22   Yet at the same time, this act of political resistance is not expressed in
23   similar terms: while some perceive their activism as either replacing or
24   indeed supporting the role of the state, others aim directly or indirectly
25   to attempt to change the sectarian elite system. For instance, when
26   asked about defining their activism, one participant summarized her
27   effort as, "Paying back to the community/ empowerment/ community
28   service/ social and political change." Her counterpart agreed, but with
29   quite different terms: "Being active / for a cause / saying "no" and not
30   accepting / translating a "no" / campaigning/ protesting /
31   demonstrating / social change / political change."

32   Indeed, supporting Karam's (2009) divisions of the civil society, two
33   types of political engagement were observed among interviewed youth
34   activists. The first type, which we classify as "system maintenance
35   practices," involves activities aiming at filling in the gaps and
36   deficiencies of the dysfunctional public services. The associations and
37   initiatives in this category include those active in social support and
38   welfare, educational campaigns, activism aiming to spread positivity

1   and generate hope. An example of a current youth-initiated program in
2   this category is LiveLoveBeirut, a crowd-sourcing campaign to spread
3   national optimism by sharing through photography the beauty of
4   Lebanon. Their recent project, livelovevolunteer.com, aims at helping
5   young Lebanese activists develop their projects, recruit volunteers, and
6   raise funds. For many, welfare and other such organizations fill an
7   important role in the quasi absence of a government. Yet as Clark and
8   Salloukh (2013) point out, system maintenance organizations reinforce
9   the political sectarian structure by filling in the gaps that the latter leave
10 behind. Once the population's basic needs are met, the urgency of a
11 political change subsides.

12   The second observed type of youth civil society are the "system
13 change practices" whereby youth activists strive directly and indirectly
14 to change the existing political system. Activists approach social change
15 in this category in two ways: as civic engagement, working within the
16 system with the aim of gradually improve it, and as civil resistance,
17 working on contesting the system through creative and alternative
18 practices. The underlying assumption among the "civil engagement"
19 group is that the original structure and set of rules in governance (the
20 existing political laws) are viable but the current practices by the
21 sectarian political class and their constituents have abused those laws.
22 Therefore, youth engage in encouraging Lebanese to abide by the rule
23 of law, call for their rights, change the way they vote (and more
24 precisely voting based on sectarian leadership), and bridge the gaps
25 between the texts and their misapplication. Associations and initiatives
26 in this sub-category are active in direct political engagements, public
27 services, political monitoring, legal activism for human and animal
28 rights, and natural ecosystem and environmental protection. Beirut
29 Madinati, for instance, ran for Beirut municipality elections in May
30 2016, presenting a group of young candidates with pro-secular, anti-
31 establishment political attitude against the sectarian-based coalition of
32 March 8 and March 14 candidates. Likewise, the Sabaa Party ran for
33 the national parliamentary elections in May 2018 promising a new
34 generation of leaders operating outside the logic of sectarianism, and a
35 vision of a civil state that is transparent and free of corruption. Out of
36 the party's 20 candidates spread across the electoral districts, one
37 running in Beirut, Paula Yacoubian, was successfully elected (The Daily
38 Star 2018).

1   On the other hand, the "civil resistance" group of youth activists
2   believe that the social distress lies in the political structure and existing
3   laws. Therefore, acts of protests and civil disobedience are called for to
4   change the political regime. A member of YouStink interviewed here
5   lists the following practices adopted by the movement during 2015
6   protests: "One, entering and taking over the Ministry of Environment;
7   two, Zebalica1, #youstink invented this symbolic weapon to shoot
8   garbage at "The Government Saray;" and three, posting grassroots
9   videos on social media to motivate people to join protests." The
10   sophistication in the performance of YouStink activists shows an
11   acquired knowledge in cultural performances (Juris 2015; Schechner
12   1993) and political campaigning. The above statement reflects the
13   range of tools activists today have at their disposal. For instance,
14   YouStink activists applied crowd mobilization and space occupation to
15   question the authority and the policies of the Ministry of Environment.
16   They strategically tried to simplify and narrow down their campaign by
17   attacking one cause (garbage as an environmental crisis) and one
18   political nemesis (the Ministry of Environment). They proposed a
19   semiotically charged performance by manipulating the signifier (the
20   garbage bags as artillery), thus creating - in the Baudrillard's (1981)
21   tradition - a new politically meaningful signifier: politicians, rather than
22   citizens, ought to live in garbage. They supported their movement with
23   a social media campaign to stimulate audience participation and
24   communicate their alternative, anti-mainstream messages. For many of
25   the activists interviewed, in fact, YouStink created a starting point for
26   a new phase of communication-savvy Lebanese activism, away from
27   traditional approaches.

28   Despite the variety of practices understood within the broader
29   purpose of political resistance, we notice that youth activists work
30   tends to system maintenance more than civil resistance. The latter is
31   called for mainly in response to specific political crises. In fact, few
32   political resistance activities took place after the 2015 waste crisis - until
33   October 2019. Beirut Madinati called for sit-ins to save Beirut public
34   beach in March 2017 (The Daily Star 2017a). Activists from different
35   civil society movements planned rallies in April 2017 opposing the
36   extension of the Lebanese parliament and calling for a new election
37   law. The civil pressure ended by having the president canceling the vote
38   for extension and pushing for the writing of a new law (Daily Star
39   2017b). This finding supports scholars' arguments about the close

1   connection of Lebanese civil movements with its socio-historical
2   context (Karam 2006; Haddad 2017) and the perceived reactionary
3   tendency of activists' political campaigns (Hermez 2011; Sukarieh
4   2007). Yet, further inspection of the activists own understandings of
5   the nature of their struggles and the potential vectors for successful
6   claim-making demonstrate a more nuanced approach that seems to
7   take seriously the particularities of the sectarian system and entrenched
8   elite politics and how to achieve successful change.

Focused Battles: The Social as the Field of Political Change

11 As emerged during interviews, in spite of open calls by activists for
12 political regime change, few believed in the successful outcome of a
13 direct and general contestation movement. Indeed, prior to 2019,
14 activists aiming for political change in Lebanon tended to avoid calling
15 for civil disobedience against the State and the political class,
16 addressing their claims instead within the boundaries of the
17 constitution. This political discourse of addressing the particular, rather
18 than the whole, is premeditated and strategic. Based on their experience
19 in the field, activists believe that if they attack the State (*"el dawle"*), that
20 represents the sectarian/confessional leaders, their message will be
21 diluted. Unlike other Arab authoritarian regimes with one head of state,
22 one focal point, Lebanon has many heads. In fact, as many scholars
23 have argued, the "stickiness" of the dominant regime is deeply
24 ideological rooted in what Dawahare (2000) calls - using Ibn
25 Khaldoun's term - sectarian *assabiya,* or strong religious identification
26 among Lebanese citizens. Within the youth activists understanding of
27 the nature of their struggles, if they attack one corrupt, underachieving
28 political leader, the latter and his party followers would directly frame
29 this act as cross-sectarian. The conflict hence would shift from issue-
30 based to a religious attack, an existential threat to the sect represented
31 by the attacked leader. Therefore, focusing political resistance on
32 specific social causes would have a higher chance of uniting Lebanese
33 of all sects.

34 This finding confirms the study of Kingston (2013), who argued
35 that youth movements in recent years have strategically decided to fight
36 particular and manageable battles, one at a time (with an accumulating,
37 long term objective of impacting social change). As Staeheli and Nagel

1   (2012, 116) note: "Throughout the Middle East and North Africa,
2   young people were mobilizing for social justice, democracy and regime
3   change, yet in Beirut they were organizing for civil marriage. It seemed
4   incongruous, to say the least." This finding also demonstrates what is
5   so radical in the October 2019 Revolution – the recognition that the
6   entire political class must be removed in order to break from the
7   entrenched system in which sectarianism and corruption are mutually
8   reinforcing.

9   ## Challenges of an Isolated Imagined Community

10   As was clear throughout the interview, the Lebanese youth activists
11   do in fact view themselves as a community apart, and as a different
12   cultural breed. Indeed, in their effort to promote change externally they
13   are also creating a safe space for themselves within the Civil Society, a
14   space where they are able to create their own ideal society internally
15   and engage only with each other. However, the convergence of "like-
16   minded people" into a community of practice has unintended negative
17   consequences. By converging inward and developing a group-think
18   mentality, the youth activists have come to realize that they are
19   diverging from their environment, losing connection with the general
20   public, and reducing influence over their constituents. They may
21   themselves be labeled as elitist and idealists. Two main tensions
22   highlight this activists-public divergence. The first relates to the
23   potential differences in concerns and priorities; the second is a cross-
24   generational tension.

25   Members of Lebanese society share overall many basic concerns
26   and worries, such as quality of public services, deteriorating financial
27   conditions, poor electricity circuits, and physical safety as well as
28   human rights issues, justice, transparency and anti-corruption. Yet,
29   Lebanon is an amalgam of different religious sects, values, cultural
30   practices, and consequently of different exigences depending on the
31   area of the country. People in the North may have different life
32   concerns and priorities from those in the South, the Bekaa Valley, or
33   from the political activist living in cosmopolitan Beirut. For instance,
34   by flagging particular human rights issues over basic survival needs of
35   food, health, shelter, or education, the political activists may not be
36   echoing the voice of local citizens. For this reason, activists fear that
37   their effort of social change is in vain. While they are attending to the

1   intellectual, cultural, and political needs of constituents, mainstream
2   political and sectarian parties are taking care of their communities' basic
3   physiological survival needs, such as food, safety and job placements.

4   The second tension between young activists and the general public
5   is cross-generational. Participants expressed an inter-generational
6   awareness comparing on one hand the youth activists with their
7   mature, established colleagues; and on the other hand, the youth
8   activists with the older generation of constituents. Inter-generational
9   differences among members were apparent in terms of positions and
10 experience. Established activists tended to describe themselves with
11 adjectives such as "committed, handworkers, and persistent/stubborn"
12 whereas youth activists framed themselves as "creative, optimists,
13 motivated, honest, and empathetic." However, this generational
14 difference is not a source of tension but rather a vehicle of transmission
15 of activism knowledge. It is a complementary coupling of the long-
16 term gratification attitude for established activists, and the short-term
17 gratification motivations of the young Lebanese activists. Many
18 participants described their effort as lacking consistency, persistence,
19 and accumulation of impact, largely because of reliance on mainly
20 young volunteers. For instance, it was noted that many of the
21 interviewed non-political organizations had a maximum of five full-
22 time members (most of them being the founders). They rely on social
23 media networks to recruit volunteers for their periodic activities.

24 For Hermez (2011) this heavy reliance of civil society on part-time
25 volunteers contributes to a pervasive culture of "reactionism" among
26 activists. Yet it is also a reflection of the competing needs and
27 responsibilities that youth activists present. Many are struggling to
28 manage between their education or profession with their side activism
29 or volunteering. According to them, their social involvement effort is
30 a necessary sacrifice of their time and financial stability. Yet they get
31 frustrated and demotivated with the perceived weak response of the
32 older generation. From the perspective of youth, the Lebanese society
33 is, as one interviewee put it, "politically biased, sectarian polarized,
34 traditional, and close-minded." The older generation is believed to be
35 more gullible to the propaganda of sectarianism adopted by
36 mainstream political leaders. The older generation, according to them,
37 is reinforcing sectarianism by electing consistently the same corrupt
38 leaders. On the other hand, the young activists are framed by the older

1   generation as a group of excited, westernized idealists. It seems that the
2   generation that went through the pain and uncertainties of the
3   Lebanese civil war is afraid to bet on a group of politically novice, risk-
4   takers.

What Possible Alternative Political Dynamic?

6   In the years leading up to the October 2019 Revolution, the youth
7   activists approach focused on specific campaigns with specific
8   objectives as well as an incremental approach to achieving political
9   change. "Build momentum through small victories," one interviewee
10 from Beirut Madinati stated. A fellow activist agreed, "Persistence is
11 key. Change is incremental!" with another emphasizing the need to
12 "build and maintain pressure on decision-makers." This culminated
13 perhaps with the establishment of Beirut Madinati to provide an
14 alternative to the political status quo through engaging in the
15 municipality elections, providing urban support (sustainability) to
16 neighborhoods in Beirut, and establishing public areas for open
17 discussions. As one interviewee from the group explained,

18   In the summer of 2015, it was the climax of civil society
19   movements. Protests were happening. Everybody was talking
20   about what could be done. The center of all manifestations was
21   the Municipality Elections of Beirut. We wanted to take action,
22   not just say no. We wanted to improve the life in the city of
23   Beirut. We gathered in December. We were 120 people. We
24   prepared presentations. Most of us were activists already. Beirut
25   Madinati was founded.

26 But while youth activists in the years leading up to 2019 were trying
27 to keep their fight issue-based, or more local through municipal-level
28 work, they faced a general public more interested in populist rhetoric
29 condemning the political system. Hence, activism was caught in the
30 tension of the particular versus the general, attacking particular social
31 causes versus attacking the whole political regime. For instance,
32 YouStink activists who coordinated the protests of 2015 were planning
33 to keep the discourse of the campaign framed as an environmental
34 crisis and focused on the Ministry of the Environment. Indeed, putting
35 public pressure on the minister to resign was their mobilization
36 objective. In their own understanding of the vectors for achieving
37 systemic change, reaching this target would give them the momentum

1   and confidence to attack other social problems, adopting a domino
2   chain effect of political change. However, controlling the campaign
3   message proved very difficult to achieve once the protest grew into a
4   mass popular movement and other political parties joined the protests
5   and started attacking the State, adding other exigent problems to their
6   list of demands. As another example, in December 2017 animal rights
7   activists protested the killing of stray dogs in a municipality at the
8   suburb of Beirut. As one interviewee recalls, protesters were
9   approached by people in the neighborhood stating, "Why should we
10   care about dogs when there's a million problems plaguing the
11   country!!"

12   More broadly, the efforts by the youth activists in the years
13   preceding 2019 to achieve meaningful change faced what they
14   perceived to be a credibility gap. Young political activists were carefully
15   avoiding being tagged as politically naïve or novice – and hence
16   untrustworthy of handling public services. In their discourse, they were
17   proposing "optimism" and "hope" as alternative to the regime's
18   discourse of sectarian polarization and fear. In their political resistance
19   practices, civil society activists strove to differentiate themselves from
20   the street thugs and political party loyals who frequently express their
21   disagreements in the street by destroying public property, burning tires,
22   blocking traffic, or raiding neighborhoods of opposing parties (see for
23   example, Bakri and Fattah 2007). Yet they also failed to develop solid
24   and well-defined political platforms. As one interviewee expressed
25   following the failed electoral bid of 2018, "Come up with actual
26   proposals/solutions: avoid just saying NO!"

27   ## Conclusion

28   In the years between 2011-2019, to what extent did the imagined
29   Civil Society of Lebanese youth activists represent a force of political
30   contestation? While the activists themselves viewed their various forms
31   of engagements as acts of political resistance, unpacking this self-
32   understanding reveals complex ideas regarding their group identity and
33   how they viewed the vectors to achieving meaningful and profound
34   political change. On one hand, the activists considered themselves a
35   "different cultural breed," seeking through their activism to live outside
36   the messy, dysfunctional, and corrupt system and produce an idealized
37   Lebanese society. And while their refuge into the Civil Society allowed

1   them to prefigure this society internally, the degree to which it was
2   being put forth externally was harder to pinpoint. While they claimed
3   to want to change the sectarian system, their content of their actions
4   and engagement only rarely addressed this directly. Instead of direct
5   political protest, they adopted specific and - importantly – less
6   confrontational strategies that were meant to break past the sectarian
7   political reality. This included focusing on social issues and not political
8   elites, projecting a sense of national identification, and working to
9   achieve electoral success through new non-sectarian political forces.
10   These various efforts, however, proved to only have limited or
11   ephemeral success in achieving this deeper goal of profound change. It
12   is within this backdrop that we can then assess what is revolutionary
13   about the October 2019 Revolution.

14   ## Bibliography

15   Allagui, Ilham and Johanne Kuebler. 2011. "The Arab Spring and the Role of
16   ICTs." *International Journal of Communication* 5: 1435-1442.
17   Anderson, Benedict. 1991. *Imagined Communities.* London: Verso.
18   Baudrillard, Jean. 1981. *Simulacres et Simulation.* Paris: Galilée.
19   Cavatorta, Francesco. 2012. "The Arab Spring: The Awakening of Civil
20   Society: A General Overview." *IEMed Mediterranean Yearbook 2012.* 75-81.
21   Clark, Janine A. and Bassel F. Salloukh. 2013. "Elite Strategies, Civil Society,
22   and Sectarian Identities in Postwar Lebanon. *International Journal of Middle*
23   *East Studies* 45, no.4: 731-749.
24   Corsaro, William A. 2005. *The Sociology of Childhood.* Thousand Oaks: Pine
25   Forge Press.
26   El-Husseini, Hashem, Stefan Toepler, and Lester M. Salamon. 2004.
27   "Lebanon." In *Global Civil Society: Dimensions of the Nonprofit Sector* edited by
28   Lester M. Salamon, S. Wojciech Sokolowski, and Associates. (Volume
29   Two). Bloomfield, CT: Kumarian Press, p. 227–232.
30   Fadda-Conrey, Carol N. 2010. "Writing Memories of the Present: Alternative
31   Narratives about the 2006 Israeli War on Lebanon." *College Literature* 37,
32   no. 1: 159–173.
33   Haddad, Tania. 2017. "Analysing State–Civil sSciety Associations
34   Relationship: The Case of Lebanon." *Voluntas* 28: 1742-1761.
35   Haugbolle, Sune. 2007. "From A-List to Webtifada: Developments in the
36   Lebanese Blogosphere 2005-2006." *Arab Media & Society.* Accessed 09
37   March 2021 https://www.arabmediasociety.com/from-a-lists-to-
38   webtifadas-developments-in-the-lebanese-blogosphere-2005-2006/
39   Juris, Jeffrey S. 2015. "Embodying Protest: Culture and Performance within
40   Social Movement." In *Anthropology, Theatre and Development: The*

Transformative Potential of Performance, edited by Alex Flynn and Jonas Tinius. London: Palgrave Macmillan, p. 82– 104.

Karam, Karam. 2006. Le Mouvement Civil au Liban: Revendications, Protestations et Mobilisations Associatives dans l'Après-Guerre. Paris: Karthala Edition.

Karam, Karam. 2009. "An Analysis of Political Change in Lebanon in the Light of Recent Mobilization Cycles." In *The Arab State and Neo-Liberal Globalization: The Restructuring of State Power in the Middle East*, edited by Laura Guazzone and Daniela Pioppi. Reading: Ithaca Press, p. 47–72.

Kingston, Paul W. 2013. Reproducing Sectarianism: Advocacy Networks and the Politics of Civil Society in Postwar Lebanon. New York: State University of New York Press.

Khalil, Joe F. 2012. "Youth-Generated Media: A Case of Blogging and Arab Youth Cultural Politics." *Television & New Media* 14, no. 4: 338-350.

Khalil, Joe F. 2017. Lebanon's Waste Crisis: An Exercise of Participation Rights. *New Media & Society* 19, no. 5: 701-712.

Kraidy, Marwan M. 2016. "Trashing the Sectarian System? Lebanon's "You Stink" Movement and the Making of Affective Publics." Communication and the Public 1, no. 1: 19-26.

Marchetti, Raffaele and Nathalie Tocci. 2009. "Conflict Society: Understanding the Role of Civil Society in Conflict." *Global Change, Peace and Security* 21, no. 2: 201–217.

Nasr, A. 2011. "Pirate Radio Stations (Lebanon)." In *Encyclopedia of Social Movement Media*, edited by John D.H. Downing DH, Thousand Oaks, CA: SAGE, p. 402–404.

Schechner, R. (1993). The Future of Ritual: Writings on Culture and Performance. London: Routledge.

Staeheli, Lynn and Caroline R. Nagel. 2012. "Whose Awakening Is It? Youth and the Geopolitics of Civic Engagement in the 'Arab Awakening.'" *European Urban and Regional Studies* 20, no. 1: 115-119.

The Daily Star 2017a. "Beirut Madinati protests ongoing works in Ramlet al-Baida." March 3, 2017.

The Daily Star 2017b. "Protests Cancelled after Parliament Session Halted." April 12, 2017.

The Daily Star 2018. "Sabaa Party Announces Candidates." March 12, 2018.

El-Amine, Adnan and Kamal Abouchedid. "Education and Citizenship: Concepts, Attitudes, Skills, and Actions. Analysis of Survey Results of 9th grade Students in Lebanon." *The National Human Development Report*. Beirut: United Nations Development Program (UNDP).

SYRIAN REVOLUTIONARY YOUTH: THE LOST AND FOUND OF POLITICAL AGENCY

Hadia Kawekji

With the cracking open of the political and civic space in 2011, Syrian youth were afforded the rare opportunity to emerge as direct and legitimately recognized political actors – something which had been denied them under the decades of repression of the Assad regime. First assuming the role of revolutionary vanguard and leading the protest movements calling for the downfall of the regime, the experience of Syrian youth in political representation was further honed through the formation of revolutionary councils. Yet despite this, Syrian youth were quickly sidelined as political actors. The revolutionary councils became isolated by institutions established by traditional elites, while young people themselves began delegating the representation of their demands to those more experienced in political affairs. This loss of representation, along with frustration with the actions (or lack thereof) of the international community, generated disillusionment among Syrian youth who had been passionate about the cause of political change. These dynamics, in turn, pushed youth revolutionaries to re-direct their activism towards local councils.

For those who made the move from revolutionary activity to work in local councils, though, this new form of engagement was not considered a practice of politics. Rather, they understood their work in the local councils as a form of community aid and humanitarian emergency work only. In other words, despite their direct involvement in local politics and their lived experience in local governance, these cadre of youth interpreted real political practice as laying in a different realm altogether, and specifically at the official international level such as in the negotiation process through Geneva or Astana.

Using an oral history approach, based on more than 30 qualitative interviews and two focus group discussions carried out from 2017-2018 with Syrian youth who moved from revolutionary activism to engagement with local councils, this paper explores the various factors

1   that contributed to the loss of representational capacity and their
2   eventual exclusion from formal political roles in the negotiation
3   process. This approach reveals both the historical reasons behind the
4   sidelining of Syrian youth as political actors but also the subjective
5   impact on them and how their own feelings of illegitimacy in the formal
6   political sphere have contributed to the loss of representation. In so
7   doing, the oral history approach also reveals a highly spatially ordered
8   understanding of where politics can and does take place. As such, the
9   paper contributes to broader knowledge on the role of Syrian youth in
10   political processes since 2011 by shedding new light on both the
11   external and internal processes of exclusion.

12   **Syrian Youth under Assad Rule: Political Drought and Avenues**
13   **for Community Action**

14   In the pre-independence era, youth formed the backbone of
15   political life, establishing active blocs and social movements that would
16   later evolve into political coalitions in post-independence Syria. Indeed,
17   youth political engagement continued until the Assad regime took
18   power in 1971, when comprehensive measures were carried out to
19   eliminate political life in the country. Hafez al-Assad took control
20   (Othman 2012) and initiated his reign by dissolving all political parties
21   except those included in the National Progressive Front (NPF). His
22   aim was to contain opposition parties under single-party rule. Assad
23   also rendered popular organizations and councils, and even the
24   People's Assembly, mere "tools in the hands of the Regional
25   Command of the Baath Party," (Dib 2014, 343) not permitted to
26   directly address any political affairs. By excluding people from
27   participation in political life, the regime was creating apolitical
28   generations of youth.

29   Assad used military and security institutions to maintain his rule,
30   terrorizing the Syrian public, spreading panic among dissidents, and
31   expanding the security/intelligence apparatus (Batatu 1999). This
32   contributed to perpetuating his rule for 30 years, and enabled him to
33   bequeath power after his death in June 2000 to his son, Bashar al-
34   Assad. Although initially embarking on some degree of economic,
35   social, and technological liberalization, which raised young people's
36   optimism during a period referred to as the Damascus Spring (Carsten
37   2012) by late 2001 a new campaign of arrests and closure of civic space
38   was again in place. Syria returned to its state of political drought, with

1 the exception of a few bold attempts towards democratic change, such
2 as the Kurdish uprising of 12 March 2004 and the Damascus
3 Declaration of 2005, which was suppressed a mere two weeks after its
4 first conference.

5 However, for those interviewed here, such crackdowns failed to
6 quash attempts by young people to organize themselves outside of
7 State-sanctioned spaces. On the contrary, Syrian youth only grew more
8 ambitious and persistent in their pursuit of democracy and engagement
9 in decision-making and public affairs. Their ambition was manifested
10 through the electoral experiences conducted by student bodies in
11 universities. It was also manifested in the proliferation of community-
12 based initiatives organized by young people, striving to shift public
13 awareness or organize community action. According to one young man
14 from Aleppo, in the era of Bashar al-Assad before the revolution:

15 "Young people's participation in Aleppo fell into two categories,
16 the first strived for reform through social and humanitarian charities,
17 sanctioned and controlled by the regime, and the other sought to work
18 in politics and thus joined the Baath Party, as the only umbrella under
19 which political action was available without the threat of arrest or
20 murder. In this way, many young people joined the ruling party despite
21 their lack of faith in the party itself."

22 Indeed, the number of youth initiatives in the field of humanitarian
23 work reflected thirst for reform in the areas of social justice and
24 development. The regime's attitude was to overlook humanitarian,
25 religious, or relief work, loosening controls and oversight by security
26 agencies. This stood in contrast to activities and initiatives of an
27 intellectual, awareness-raising or even educational orientation, which
28 were met with strict security by a regime that sought to suppress any
29 movement that could affect its hold over power. In other words, in the
30 period preceding the revolution, the regime adopted a policy of turning
31 a blind eye to youth action in community-based initiatives, either
32 because of a belief that they could be managed or controlled, or
33 because the regime did not see them as a threat.

34 In their collective narrative, the third millennium saw several factors
35 intersect that raised youth interest in political action that could impact
36 national decision-making. This includes the programs of economic
37 liberalization and technological openness at the local level, and the

1   invasion of Iraq at the regional level. One young activist described this
2   period in his hometown of Homs by saying:

3   "To some extent, there was a political awareness and involvement
4   in public affairs. During the period of 2005-2010, civil society
5   associations became active in Homs, encouraging young people to join
6   community action (such as the provision of education and health
7   support to the poor and to families in marginalized areas). There was
8   also mobilization around governmental reform, anti-corruption, and
9   social justice. This was especially the case of the Islamist movement
10 (Salafists and Hizb ut-Tahrir). Great mobilization took place against
11 the regime at the time, and the latter met it with repression and arrests.
12 In the second half of that decade, the regime allowed some parties from
13 the NPF, such as the SSNP and the Communist Party, to conduct
14 organized action, as parties of the NPF were controlled by the security
15 and the ruling party. This encouraged many young people who wished
16 to engage in political activity outside Baath Party frameworks to be
17 involved in the two parties, where the youth found a relatively free
18 space for political engagement in national and other causes."

19   Meanwhile, the regime's goal was to find a containable outlet
20 through which to channel young people's aspirations for political
21 engagement, and thereby prevent the formation of any real opposition.
22 As a young activist from Deir ez-Zor said:

23   "The Assad regime staffed key positions in government directorates
24 and departments with members of the Alawite sect whom it had
25 recruited from the Syrian coast. This caused a great deal of unrest
26 against the regime, especially among young university graduates, which
27 increased dramatically in the years leading up to the revolution."

28   In Idlib, for instance, the situation was particularly tense, especially
29 in Ma'arat al-Nu'man. Before the revolution, several attempts were
30 made by young men to mobilize against the regime – notably by Jund
31 al-Sham in 2008-2009, as recounts one activist from Idlib. These
32 attempts rendered the regime's security grip tighter in the area, and
33 increased local fears of any gathering of young men, especially in
34 mosques. Meanwhile, rural Damascus saw several youth initiatives for
35 reform, including the Darayya Youth Group in 2003, which aimed at
36 social reform and sowed the seeds of a genuine civil movement
37 independent of the regime. However, the initiative ended with broad

1   arrests targeting its organizers, according to an interviewee from
2   Damascus.

3   In the city of Damascus, one activist attributed the lack of political
4   life in the capital to the tighter security controls than those in rural
5   areas, thereby allowing rural Damascene areas such Al-Tall, Douma,
6   and Wadi Barada to emerge as more propitious political environments.
7   Nonetheless, despite the severe security grip in the capital, social
8   initiatives in Damascus were reflected in various youth attempts at
9   political association, such as the secret meetings of members of the
10   Damascus Declaration, as well as meetings in the homes of public
11   figures who opposed the regime in private or in public. The capital also
12   saw the establishment of small secret youth political forums, which
13   would meet in coffee shops periodically and whose members would
14   later join the SSNP.

15   The introduction and spread of the internet during Bashar al-
16   Assad's era contributed to the formation of virtual associations and
17   forums, and facilitated communication among young people in
18   preparation for the revolutionary movement. Riding the wave of the
19   Arab Spring, Syrian youth began to gather under various groups that
20   began organizing the peaceful protest movement, launching slogans for
21   the Fridays of protest through social media, and calling for gatherings
22   and protests to express popular demands in March 2011 (Asharq Al-
23   Awsat 2012). Peaceful demonstrations soon began to spread
24   throughout the country, ultimately becoming a mass revolution and a
25   public culture in which even commercial markets participated through
26   strikes, thus responding to calls by the revolutionary youth and
27   challenging the brutal security crackdown on the movement –
28   especially in the cities.

29   **From Revolutionary Vanguard to Loss of Representation**

30   In the March 2011 revolution, Syrian youth encountered a
31   newfound hope of changing their economic, social, and political
32   realities on the one hand, and their positionality vis-à-vis the national
33   decision-making process on the other. The first year of the revolution
34   was characterized by bottom-up political structures, which emanated
35   from the grassroots level and assumed higher political roles. In the
36   second year of the revolution, however, these structures began to wane
37   in favor of other political opposition entities created by the previous

1 generation of traditional political actors and elites. These emergent
2 opposition bodies only held minor or tokenistic representation of
3 youth groups, which at that stage lacked international connections
4 compared with old opposition figures in exile. Moreover, the lack of
5 representation was borne out of young people's own perception of
6 their inadequate experience and capacities in the political arena, and
7 their dearth of practical political experience after decades of political
8 repression. This led to the exclusion of young people from political
9 practice, as well as the disillusionment of youth themselves towards the
10 political path of the revolution, which further repelled them from it.

11 From the perspective of interviewees participating in the protest
12 movements in 2011, the crucial motor behind revolutionary activity
13 was the cohort born in the 1990s. In their recounting, revolutionary
14 youth organized themselves into virtual blocs in larger cities, and into
15 more concrete associations in rural areas and closed social
16 environments, a difference in organizational style that reflected the
17 different degrees of security surveillance and repression (Askif 2012).
18 Rural-based revolutionary activity was characterized by large
19 gatherings, ease of movement and the retention of social ties and
20 relations, compared to cities where large internal migration had led to
21 a disintegration of social fabric. Furthermore, urban dwellers depended
22 heavily on State-censored public means of communication (wired and
23 wireless), which were less common in rural areas and governorates far
24 from the capital, especially in marginalized areas. According to an
25 activist from Daraa, the harsh nature of rural life, which is more
26 conducive to boldness than life in the city where more amenities are
27 available, the concentration of a segment of the population familiar
28 with the criminality of the Assad regime, and the less securitized
29 presence of the regime in the countryside, were all factors that
30 contributed to denser and broader protest movement in the
31 countryside than in the cities early in the revolution.

32 With the passage of the first weeks of revolution – the second
33 quarter of 2011 – revolutionary political structures began to emerge
34 under the name of Coordination Committees (CCs) and Syrian
35 Revolution Coordinators Union (SRCU), which were mostly rooted in
36 their geographic locations (a CC for each district/town/city, etc.). At
37 that stage, no political revolutionary discourse readily existed, and the
38 youths' focus was on voicing their fundamental demands for freedom,

1   dignity, justice, and the expression of political will. As the regime's
2   brutality escalated in suppressing the protests, though, so did the
3   demands, which culminated in the pursuit of the fall of the regime (Al-
4   Alou 2018).

5   With the consolidation and proliferation of the protest movement
6   across Syria, these revolutionary structures began to rapidly evolve and
7   allowed for an expansion of the youth activists' political skills-set. This
8   included meetings with local, regional, and international political
9   figures to develop discourse, requesting financial, informational, or
10   technical support, and seeking strategic guidance for revolutionary
11   mobilization. Yet while these youth activists of the CCs were at the
12   helm of the revolutionary movement, they also supported external
13   political entities who represented them internationally. Indeed, the
14   enhanced coordination between the youth of the revolutionary
15   movement and veteran opposition voices in exile, leading to the
16   inception of the National Coordination Committee for Democratic
17   Change (NCC) in June of 2011, saw the youth activists move backstage.
18   The role of the revolutionary movement was thus transformed into
19   mere support for those older opposition figures. For the youth activists
20   interviewed here, this loss of representation of the revolutionary
21   movement represented a critical turning point. In allowing
22   representation to be undertaken by others, youth embarked on a path
23   of diminishing engagement in political practice and an inability to keep
24   pace with accelerating international developments. With the passage of
25   time, this led to the widening of the gap between revolutionary youth
26   and the older generation of the political opposition.

27   This process continued with the formation of the Syrian National
28   Council (SNC) in August 2011. For the activists interviewed here, the
29   emergence of the SNC signaled the onset of a series of errors, which
30   began by placing emphasis on traditional opposition figures who
31   enjoyed media presence or belonged to historically political families in
32   Syria – at the expense of youth. At the time, the revolutionary scene
33   reflected a spontaneous mandate granted to political elites by the
34   popular mobilization, exhibiting the lack of awareness of the risk of
35   political exclusion of young people, both from the revolutionary
36   movement itself and from the political elites that later spearheaded the
37   scene. This was perhaps most evident in the words of one of the
38   founders of the SNC, who addressed the revolutionary movement by

1   saying: "We left the street to you, leave politics to us (Atassi 2018)."

2   In parsing their narration of this period, the spontaneous mandate
3   of representation granted by the youth activists to traditional
4   opposition entities can be explained by two factors. The first is the
5   security conditions and the difficulty of mobilizing youth in areas under
6   regime control and, more importantly, intensified arrest campaigns
7   targeting young men and aimed at their detention or recruitment in the
8   regime's military. This crackdown led to the dispersal of young
9   revolutionary leaders, many of whom were detained, killed, or self-
10   exiled in fear of a similar fate. Meanwhile, those who remained
11   concealed their real identities for fear of reprisals by the security forces
12   targeting their families in regime-controlled areas. In light of growing
13   needs, on the other hand, activists on the ground faced a depletion of
14   their financial and human resources: in responding to humanitarian
15   needs, revolutionary youth were diverted in terms of their activities and
16   saw financial support to the revolution go instead to relief efforts.

17   Just as importantly, though, were the subjective perceptions held by
18   young people. As comes across in the interviews, youth activists were
19   convinced of the sanctity of revolutionary work and maintained that
20   any political ambition at that stage would be a manifestation of greed
21   and an attempt to prematurely reap the fruits of a revolution that had
22   yet to meet popular demands (Bishara 2013). As such, youth activists
23   deliberately shied away from political activities and instead focused on
24   maintaining revolutionary momentum. Moreover, many viewed
25   themselves as politically inadequate and lacking in tools and experience
26   and thus unable to lead a political entity that may compete against an
27   internationally recognized State. There was thus a natural deference to
28   exiled dissidents who had developed more political resilience in terms
29   of mobility, media presence, and networking with internationally
30   influential figures.

31   This loss of representation and agency would be compounded by
32   the youth activists' own disillusionment with the formal peace
33   negotiation process and the shift away from the UN-sponsored
34   Geneva process and towards the Russia-sponsored militarized Astana
35   track. While the formation of the High Negotiations Committee
36   (HNC) in 2015 to unify the Syrian opposition was initially greeted with
37   considerable support, the unstable international climate and the great
38   losses incurred by the rebels in 2016 rendered it incapable of meeting

1   revolutionary demands (Al-Hafiz 2018). Furthermore, the Sochi
2   Conference was received with overwhelming popular discontent and
3   demands to boycott its outcomes, in particularly because of repeated
4   failure to meet any of the promises made internationally to stop the
5   brutal bombing of civilians. All of these elements led to great alienation
6   of youth revolutionaries towards their negotiating body, and further
7   undermined its credibility to represent them. To this point, many youth
8   revolutionary activists stopped following news of the political
9   opposition and refused to join their ranks for fear of losing their
10   "revolutionary credibility." Others were cautious so as not to bear
11   responsibility for the poor performance of the political opposition. On
12   the other hand, revolutionary youths opted out of political
13   partisanship, which they viewed as exacerbating the fragmentation of
14   the popular base, opting instead for rallying people behind the
15   fundamental principles of the revolution (freedom, justice, and dignity)
16   and the one message demanding the downfall of the regime.

17   What emerged instead among certain youth revolutionary activists
18   was work within local councils. In those fora, youth found an avenue
19   to meet the basic demands for which they took to the streets early in
20   the revolution, from reclaiming their role in decision-making to
21   fulfilling the demands of the population and giving representation to
22   the most affected and least represented segments among them.

23   **Participation in Local Councils: A Truncated Agency?**

24   The advent of the militarization phase of the revolution in late 2011
25   saw the liberation of some territories, the withdrawal of State services,
26   and a natural development of local political structures. As the
27   revolutionary youth activists undertook relief efforts in areas targeted
28   by the regime, they also sought, from within the emergent local
29   structures, to fulfill service needs such as healthcare, education, water
30   and sanitation, and civil registration, among others. With time, these
31   evolved into civil bodies that served local populations and aimed to
32   administer non-regime held (or "liberated") areas. They became known
33   as the local councils, and the majority of their staff were comprised of
34   the revolutionary youth, as recounted during focus group discussions.
35   As on activist from Deir ez-Zor explained,

36   "After the outbreak of the revolution, we started in 2012 working
37   in a small group of young people, which evolved into a youth group

1 whose aim was to organize the area in Deir ez-Zor. We called it the
2 Youth for Change Assembly. Its goals were serving the population and
3 organizing the liberated areas. Later on, a shift occurred towards
4 elections and choosing representatives. There was an opposition TV
5 channel that we communicated with to relay the voices of the
6 population and the message of our assembly. This was the first non-
7 partisan youth organization. We had an idea of transforming into a
8 political party but it was rejected because the political moment was not
9 suitable for partisanship."

10 The local councils formed a link between local populations and
11 donors who financed services, which granted these bodies a certain
12 degree of legitimacy. This legitimacy was in turn enhanced by electoral
13 or consensus-building mechanisms in the selection of their members
14 (Sharabji 2018). Remarkably, the adoption of amended Law No. 107
15 by the Ministry of Local Administration in the Syrian Interim
16 Government (SIG) and the implementation of its regulations and
17 directives provided legal reference to the eligibility and selection
18 process of local council members. The subsequent development of
19 local councils over time increased representative legitimacy, especially
20 as militarization intensified and the liberated areas expanded, in
21 conjunction with repeated attempts by armed factions to intrude into
22 civic activity and intervene in public affairs. As a response, local
23 councils began exerting pressure on the factions to obstruct them from
24 the civil administration of liberated areas.

25 Over time, the local councils continued to grow out of necessity,
26 although their number has varied considerably since 2012. Some local
27 councils were forced to dissolve after the fall of their areas to Assad's
28 army, or were displaced and forced to operate in exile, often merging
29 with other councils. As of 2018, the number of local councils was
30 estimated at 303 by the Local Administration Councils Unit, most of
31 whose members were young people who had a clear role providing
32 services and meeting livelihood needs despite inadequate financial and
33 human resources. Whether elected or selected by consensus, the
34 members of these councils kept a distance from political polarization
35 and donors' agendas and retained the status of regulator and
36 coordinator of CSOs.[1] They also played rather unrecognized political

---

[1] Although the local councils emanate from the grassroots level, it is notable that women were underrepresented in terms of membership in the elected councils, despite the presence of many

1   roles, such as representing local population, expressing their demands,
2   and keeping abreast with Syria-related international and political
3   developments while issuing statements and restating political positions
4   in the media.

5   By their own account, the revolutionary youth activists who moved
6   into the sphere of local councils do not view these as a form of political
7   practice. Politics, to their view, was restricted to the internationally
8   recognized processes such as Geneva and Astana, which they deemed
9   as deaf to the voice of the revolutionary public and heedless of its
10   thoughts about the political process. Conversely, they regarded serving
11   in local councils as a small-scale representation of local population in
12   which priority is given to service provision. This, perhaps more than
13   anything, demonstrates how young people's convictions about local
14   councils are governed by the Baathist bifurcation between public
15   service – the provision of services and the representation of people –
16   and political action – be that domestic politics and governance or
17   foreign policy. Such inherited preconceptions about public affairs
18   persisted despite the fact that awareness of governance and democracy
19   made considerable strides in the wake of the Syrian revolution,
20   especially after the experiences of genuine elections in a number of
21   local councils in liberated areas.

22   In parsing the narratives of youth activists, what becomes clear is
23   that the collective understandings of what constitutes politics and
24   political action in the post-2011 period has contributed to undermining
25   their participation in determining the political future of their country.
26   The collective understanding of the nature of local council work placed
27   emphasis on service provision only. This understanding is rooted in the
28   perception of local governance in the pre-revolution era, which had

---

women in local councils, often in the sectors of education, health and general administration. Members of the local councils participating in focus group discussions point to limited women's candidacy for local council membership. However, as recounted by participants in the focus groups, the underrepresentation of women in the local councils can be attributed to several reasons. Some are objective, such as social customs, traditions and the security situation, while other reasons are more subjective, including women's lack of confidence in their ability to work in decision-making settings and challenge a stereotypical outlook. In general, the percentage of women's participation varies according to the regions and the specificities of each governorate. While the local council of Nawa, Daraa has no representation for women, the local council of Ma'rat al-Nu'man, Idlib includes a substantial number of women as representatives or employees. This variation in the representation of women between different governorates can be explained by the tribal nature of some governorates, on the one hand, and the proximity of others to the border and their relative enjoyment of cultural openness.

1   indeed been confined to services, and subject to tight security control
2   by the Baath Party. This shared vision of local council work as detached
3   from local governance was reinforced by the realities under which local
4   councils operated, and their preoccupation primarily with the provision
5   of services to local populations in liberated areas. Moreover, only a few
6   local councils have been active at the level of engagement in the
7   international peace processes (Geneva and Astana), as most youth do
8   not believe they possess the expertise and competence to participate.
9   Additionally, a large number of youth activists as interviewed here
10 maintain the belief that the current international political process is
11 governed by the decisions and interests of conflicting major powers,
12 rather than the will of Syrians themselves. As such, any engagement in
13 politics is ultimately viewed as conducive to instrumentalization by
14 State actors involved in the Syrian conflict. As a result, the
15 revolutionary youth did not see the work of local councils as political
16 practice that could enable them to engage in the ongoing political
17 process. This has resulted, however, in a vicious circle: the lack of
18 political engagement has prevented the acquisition of experience and
19 expertise, which only further drives the feeling of inadequacy and
20 aversion to political participation. In other words, while youth through
21 the local councils conducted outright political tasks, such as local
22 negotiations, reconciliation and ceasefires, participation in protests,
23 international meetings, and issuing political statements (Arab Reform
24 Initiative 2018), they failed to translate these roles into political action
25 that would grant them presence as key actors in the international peace
26 process.

27 **Conclusion**

28 In March 2011, Syrian youth took to the streets with clearly
29 articulated popular demands in a political revolution aiming at
30 reclaiming their role in decision-making. Yet, despite young people's
31 growing interest in political affairs after the revolution, and their
32 increased awareness of the importance of participation in public affairs
33 and national decision-making, the political experience that ensued
34 failed to provide channels for absorbing activist youth. Instead, they
35 faced exclusion from engaging with emergent political bodies, resulting
36 in deep frustration, in parallel with a process of self-isolation based on
37 a belief in their own political inadequacy. This contributed to an
38 inclination towards local activism, especially in liberated areas, which

1 provided non-traditional political action within the framework of local
2 councils. Over time, however, the fall of many of these areas into the
3 regime's hands further marginalized the youth activists and restricted
4 their ability to engage even in informal political practice.

5 In conducting an oral history analysis of the revolutionary youth
6 activists' trajectories over the course of the revolution, this study has
7 illuminated the various reasons why they lost representation over the
8 movement they initially led. Youth activists moved from a position of
9 vanguard to supporting roles, and understood their domain of activity
10 as moving from the realm of politics to that of humanitarian relief. This
11 has been the result both of processes of exclusion and self-isolation,
12 leading to the marginalizing of revolutionary youth from the
13 composition of political structures, but also their own shared
14 understanding of what constitutes political action and its utility on the
15 ground in Syria in increasingly complex and dire circumstances.

16 As the years of the revolution progressed, various political
17 structures claimed political representation of the revolution, ranging
18 from the National Coordination Committee to the Syrian National
19 Council, then the National Coalition and finally the High Negotiations
20 Committee. What soon became evident, however, was the poor
21 performance of these structures and their limited ability to maintain
22 rapport with the youth activists. This was a factor of frustration for the
23 youth that led to their alienation from the ongoing political processes.
24 For interviewees, however, the protracted nature of the conflict has led
25 to a realization that their spontaneous decision to delegate political
26 representation was an error. Their lack of acknowledgement at the
27 beginning of the revolution of the importance of the political agency
28 they had earned at the moment they sparked the revolution contributed
29 to their exclusion from the official political arena and to their loss of
30 that agency. Instead, they turned towards local activism and local
31 councils, in which they exercised many political roles and thus acquired
32 a new political agency. However, they have yet to translate this agency
33 into an active political presence in the official political process. Just as
34 importantly, perhaps, is that they do not necessarily recognize this as a
35 form of political agency, failing to see the political in their work within
36 the local councils.

37 Yet in assessing their narrations, what also emerges is a tendency
38 among many to study political science. This perhaps is an indication of

their will to acquire the knowledge of political practice as well as to transform the informal political agency they acquired through local council activity into an official agency and take the lead of political action and engage in national decision-making in a future Syria.

References

al-Hafiz, Hussam. 2018. Author interview.

Al-Alou, Sasha. 2018. Political Emanations of the Syrian Revolution: Trends, Weights and Eventualities. Harmoon Center For Contemporary Studies.

Arab Reform Initiative. 2018. "Decentralization and Local Councils in Post-Conflict Syria: What Role Can Youth Play?" 31 October 2018. https://www.arab-reform.net/event/decentralization-and-local-councils-in-post-conflict-syria-what-role-can-youth-play/

Asharq Al-Awasat. 2012. "Friday Names Documented the Revolution, Made Syrians in Opposition to the Assad Rule More in Solidarity." 16 March 2012. https://archive.aawsat.com/details.asp?section=4&article=668269&issue no=12162#.YCsgSC1Q2qQ

Askif, Moayad. 2012. "Syrian Countryside Overwhelm the City. *Orient News*, 24 November 2012. https://bit.ly/2VCoFPT

Atassi, Suhair. 2018. "Who Can Sweep Away the Assad Regime? Its Fall Alone is Not Enough," *Syria TV*, 03 November 2018. https://goo.gl/hZBchj.

Hanna Batatu, Syria's Peasantry: The Descendants of its Lesser Rural Notables, and Their Politics. Princeton University Press, 1999.

Bishara, Azmi. 2013. Syria: A Path to Passion Towards Freedom: An Attempt at Contemporary Historiography. The Arab Center for Research and Policy Studies, 2013.

Carsten, Wieland. 2012. Syria – A Decade of Lost Chances: Repression and Revolution from Damascus Spring to Arab Spring. Seattle: Cune Press.

Dib, Kamal. 2012. Contemporary History of Syria: From French Mandate to Summer 2011. Dar Al-Nahar.

Othman, Hashim. 2012. *Modern History of Syria*. Beirut: Ryad Al-Rayyes.

Sharabji, Mazhar. 2018. Author interview.

IS THERE A YOUTH POLITICS?

2 Asef Bayat

3   Is there such a thing as 'youth politics' in the way we have gender
4   politics, working class politics, or poor people's politics; and if there is,
5   what are its attributes and modes of expression? After all, what is the
6   significance of youth politics, if any? Even though some have
7   expressed doubts about 'youth' as a meaningful category or considered
8   it as a mere construct, here I would like to propose an analytical lens
9   which may help understanding youth as a useful category with distinct
10   politics. In this sense 'youth politics' will be viewed in terms of the
11   conflicts and negotiations over claiming or defending youthfulness; but
12   this is a politics that is mediated by the position of the young in class,
13   gender, racial, sexual and other involved social structures. In brief, the
14   political outlook of a young person may be shaped not just by the
15   exclusive preoccupation with 'youthfulness', but also by his/her
16   positionality as citizen, poor, female, or a member of a sexual minority.
17   The propositions advanced here are informed by my observations on
18   young people's lives in the contemporary Middle East, where the
19   spectacular Arab uprisings brought youth to the forefront of politics.

20   A review of popular discourse as well as scholarly works on the
21   Arab revolutions leaves little doubt about the leading presence of the
22   young people in these momentous political episodes. Perhaps no other
23   social group has gained as much credence in these transformative
24   events as youth, and in no other times in its history has Middle East
25   politics witnessed so much attention to youth—whether as victims of
26   economic marginalization or agents of transformation. A range of
27   writings narrates the prominent role of the young and students in the
28   region's national movements and revolutions. They discuss how, for
29   instance, the indignant youth suffered from the highest rate of
30   unemployment in the world, how they moved from being passive
31   subjects into active agents, in what way the rising 'youth movements'
32   initiated the revolutions, or how the Coptic youth turned into a political
33   player in post-revolution Egypt (Abdalla 2016; Delgado 2015; Desai,
34   Olofsgard, and Yousef 2016; Erlich 2015; Sayer and Yousef 2016;

1 Shehata 2012). Indeed, the notion of 'youth revolutions' referring to
2 the Arab Spring readily pointed to an assumed propensity of youth for
3 radical politics.

4   While we have certainly learnt more about the involvement of
5 young people in politics, much of the literature displays the perennial
6 problem of treating youth simply as *incidental* or at best tangential to the
7 core stories and analyses. As such, this genre of writing discusses not
8 the youth per se, but rather such subjects of contentious politics, the
9 uprising, or activism in certain times or places in which youth happen
10 to play a key role, such that if we were to substitute youth with a
11 different group, it would have no significant bearings on the analyses
12 and narratives. At the same time, in the studies where 'youth' do take a
13 more prominent place, there are little or no discussions about the
14 specificities of youth claims and presence in such events; youth often
15 appears as a term to designate an age cohort rather than a conceptual
16 category with particular analytical meanings. In fact, many of the
17 writings on 'youth movements' are of this nature; they are not about
18 'youth movements' per se, but about certain political organizations,
19 parties, or networks—such as the Kefaya, the Egyptian democracy
20 movement of the mid-2000s—in which young people happen to be
21 active. This kind of treatment is not limited to the Middle East, but
22 seems to inform much of the literature on youth and politics in general.
23 This strand of scholarship on youth then tends to examine not *youth
24 politics* per se, but *youth in politics*. The discussions of 'youth in politics'
25 do certainly teach us a great deal about the extent to which young
26 people care about or get engaged in public life. But they say little about
27 the particularities—concerns, forms, direction, pitfalls or promises—
28 of such political engagement. For these, we need to delve into 'youth
29 politics'.

30 **In Historical Movements**

31   There is globally a sizeable scholarship that takes 'youth politics' as
32 its central focus. Here youth politics is construed from the sociological
33 reality of the young in terms of their transitional position from
34 childhood and dependence to adulthood and responsibility. While
35 some in this genre tend to view the young as emotional, inexperienced,
36 and potential instigators of 'youth war', most see them as creative
37 producers of subcultures and new lifestyles, as well as carriers of
38 revolutionary posture and politics (Amara 2012). In fact, here youth

1   appear as key players in the major political movements in history all the
2   way from Ancient Greece to the English Revolution, Protestant
3   Reformation, the early 19th Century, and down to the momentous
4   episode of the 1960s. In the inter-war period, youth as a distinct social
5   group assumed such an import as to make both the right and leftist
6   political blocks invest heavily in the transformative potential of the
7   youth. This gave rise to myriad 'youth movements' with intimate links
8   to communist or fascist ideologies and personas (Kalman 2003)
9   including Mussolini, who considered youth as the 'avant-garde of the
10   fascist revolution'(Passerini 1997). Indeed, the old idea of associating
11   youth with nature, body building, and soul searching was reincarnated
12   after the Second World War in the ministries of Youth and Sports in
13   most postcolonial nations, where a variety of 'young movements' such
14   as the Young Officers in Egypt or Young Turks in the Turkish
15   Republic ascended to the political stage (Sukarieh and Tannock 2015).

16   The historic events of the 1960s brought youth more than ever onto
17   the forefront of revolutionary politics. The student revolts in Berkeley
18   and its Free Speech Movement spreading through the US campuses,
19   together with youth and student rebellions in Europe, Latin America,
20   Africa, and Asia, and especially the May 1968 general strike in factories
21   and colleges presented the youth as if they possessed an inherent
22   radical habitus. Such notions as 'youthful rebelliousness' and 'youth
23   war' virtually linked those revolutionary moments to a youthful
24   disposition, assumed to be shaped by a specific 'stage of life', a mix of
25   alienation and presence, or the generation war (Keniston 1972; Matza
26   1961). While some argued that age conflict had taken the place of class
27   conflict (Turner 1969), others took the young as the new revolutionary
28   class that had replaced the proletariat as the agent of political
29   transformation (Rowntree and Rowntree 1968). The idea of 'youth as
30   class' and university as a new bastion of revolutionary politics
31   resonated strongly with some major social theorists ranging from
32   Jerome Ferrand, Fred Halliday, C. Wright Mills, and Hebert Marcuse.
33   For the sociologist Alain Touraine, the university came to occupy the
34   same position as the great capitalist enterprise (Touraine 1968). The
35   idea of 'revolutionary youth' also permeated into the discourse of the
36   Arab uprisings, which young people had initiated. Some observers
37   went so far as to describe key historical moments in the Middle East
38   far prior to the Arab uprisings in terms of the revolutionary role of
39   youth. As 'an age group and as an educated public', youth and students

1   are suggested to have burst into the political scene to shape nationalist
2   movements, liberation struggles, and revolutions, as well as Islamism
3   and liberalism (Erlich 2015).

4   A longitudinal look at the young people's behavior, however, would
5   make the claims of 'radical youth' untenable. Young people, whether
6   in the West or in the Middle East, have also exhibited both passive and
7   conservative orientations. It is well known that the political youth of
8   the 1960s and 1970s in the US and Britain turned by the 1980s into
9   Yuppies or the self-absorbed and conservative young professionals—
10   orientations very different from the working class punk subculture. For
11   their part, Arab youth went through a process of hibernation for
12   decades before joining the 2011 uprisings; young people in Tunisia
13   were constricted by the police state under the Ben Ali, and those in
14   Egypt showed little interest during the 1990s in any sort of civic
15   activism let alone revolutionary politics, if they had not joined the
16   Islamist Jihadi fringes. Large-scale surveys of Arab youth conducted
17   after the 2011 revolutions point to an escalating apathy and aversion to
18   politics following an earlier political fervor that marked the uprisings
19   (Friedrich Ebert Stiftung 2017). In fact, some observers have
20   concluded that Arab youth usually display apathy when it comes to the
21   conventional politics, political parties, or elections, simply because of
22   their deep disenchantment with formal intuitions. Yet the very same
23   passive youth may turn political in particular political circumstances,
24   such as during the Arab uprisings (Desai, Olofsgard, and Yousef 2016).

25   **From Passive to Active**

26   Why and how do the young turn from passive individuals into active
27   and even revolutionary agents? More specifically, how do we explain
28   the widespread political turn among the Arab youth in the 2011 events?
29   One suggestion is that youth apathy changes when their discontent
30   rises so high that they resort to radical and dramatic action with
31   perceived impact on government and cost to themselves (Desai,
32   Olofsgard, and Yousef 2016). Here the sources of discontent are
33   invariably attributed to a series of misfortunes, chiefly exclusion and
34   unemployment. Thus, in the common narrative, the Arab world's
35   highest youth unemployment—25% compared to world average
36   14.4% in pre-revolution—meant late marriage (until 30s) and
37   'waithood', leading to frustration and ultimately revolt (Sayer and
38   Yousef 2016; Shehata 2016).

1   There is certainly a great plausibility in these narratives, in particular
2   when it comes to uncertainty and 'waithood', which indeed appear to
3   be mostly youth problems. But broadly speaking, unemployment and
4   economic and social exclusion are hardly the exclusive predicament of
5   the young; adults have also suffered from these misfortunes. But if the
6   focus is on youth, what type of youth we are speaking about—college
7   students, graduates, rich, poor, those living with parents, or married
8   young couples who must rely on themselves? The youth of the rich and
9   privileged families are not supposed to feel social and economic
10   exclusion, and should not, by definition, be outraged and rebellious.
11   Studies on the economics of Middle Eastern youth show that family
12   income has the greatest bearing on young people's educational
13   opportunities, achievements, and eventually income; the more well-off
14   the family is, the better chance for better degrees and opportunities
15   (Salehi-Esfahani 2016). Even those non-privileged high school or
16   college students (in a 2016 survey 37% of youth between 16-30 years
17   of age were students) (Friedrich Ebert Stiftung 2017) who do live with
18   and depend on parents may not experience the hardship of
19   unemployment or economic exclusion as long as they remain outside
20   of job market; it is their parents who in their role as providers for these
21   youngsters should feel the crunch of socio-economic exclusion. Unlike
22   in, say, the US or Britain, where the autonomous youth depend mostly
23   on themselves to subsist, in Arab societies it is the families that usually
24   bear the burden of youths, sometimes even after their children get
25   married (see Friedrich Ebert Stiftung 2017. Aspects of this pattern have
26   emerged recently in the countries hit by financial crisis such as Spain
27   and Greece, where youth unemployment has resulted in diminishing
28   parents' pension funds). In other words, the economic pressure falls
29   more on parents than on their children, and thus it is these parents who
30   should be rebelling. This might explain why a large number of the
31   young respondents (71%) in the MENA youth survey described their
32   economic situation as 'good' despite the relative economic downturn,
33   because these young people were living on their parents' income
34   (Friedrich Ebert Stiftung 2017). However, married couples who were
35   responsible for their own household did complain about the pressure
36   of bad economic conditions.

37   A year before the Egyptian Revolution, the veteran columnist
38   Hasan Nafaa published a piece in *Al-Masry Al-Youm* where he
39   suggested that new social actors were emerging onto Egypt's political

1 scene (Nafaa 2010). He described three occasions where young people
2 (with work and families) approached him to start a campaign to change
3 the political status quo in Egypt—to support the opposition leader
4 Mohamed Baradei, endorse groups demanding to amend the
5 constitution, and help them push the parliament to reform things.
6 Nafaa then suggested that we are facing a new category of youth in
7 their 30s and 40s who hold responsibilities for their nuclear families as
8 parents and for their jobs in public and private sectors; these youth are
9 inclined not for revolution to alter everything, but towards cooperation
10 and peaceful, managed change. These young activists, he argued, were
11 different from the radical students of the 1970s or those in the April
12 6th Youth Movement in Egypt. These youth were not simply interested
13 in their own individual or family matters, but were also concerned
14 about the public good. Deeply worried about the failure of the state,
15 they wanted to do something about it; they sensed that the alarming
16 situation could lead to an explosion, especially when neither the regime
17 nor the traditional opposition were able to bring about reforms. 'I do
18 not think I exaggerate in stating', Nafaa concluded, 'that the advent of
19 this new age cohort (generation) in the political stage constitutes a
20 turning point in mobilization for change'.

21

22 **Who are Youth?**

23 This interesting observation raises serious conceptual questions
24 about and complicates the meaning of youth and youth political
25 agency. Can one consider this 30-40 year-old age cohort with marriage,
26 work and responsibility 'youth'? Is 'youth' simply an age-category? Is it
27 simply a construction imagined and presented by others? Or is there
28 no such thing as 'youth' at all? The policy circles such as the United
29 Nations Development Program (UNDP) usually define youth in terms
30 of certain age groups—some take it as those 15-25 year of age, others
31 15-30, while others up to 40 (UNDP 2016). Even though
32 operationalization is necessary for policy purposes, such designations
33 with varied ranges remain inevitably arbitrary. It is therefore not a
34 surprise that some scholars reject the category of 'youth' in terms of
35 'life stage' and or in terms of generation altogether, considering it
36 instead as a 'construction'—a social identity that is imagined by others
37 about the young (Sukarieh and Tannock 2014). But this is no less

1   problematic. It is true that elders, the state, or moral authorities do
2   intervene to construct different images of youth as, for instance,
3   'rebellious', 'brave', the 'future', or 'dangerous'. This however does not
4   mean that youth lack any reality of their own. Perhaps we should be
5   asking how the young define themselves; for this can help us to identify
6   those particular traits that, beyond external attributions, shape young
7   people's image of themselves and their behavior. Denying the young
8   the ability to define their own reality, or overlooking their paradoxical
9   positionality in the social structure, can lead to such inaccurate
10   conclusions that, as Bourdieu put is, youth is 'nothing but a word'.

11   I have suggested that 'youth' in the sense of young persons is in part
12   related to a particular life stage and thus a particular location in the
13   social structure, where the individuals navigate between the world of
14   childhood (as the time of vulnerability, innocence and need of
15   protection) and adulthood, the world of work and responsibility.
16   Theoretically, a young person experiences a life of relative autonomy,
17   a kind of 'structural irresponsibility', where the individual neither
18   substantially depends on other people such as parents, nor is
19   responsible for others, such as his/her own family or children. This
20   seems to be in line with the perceptions of young Egyptians who, in
21   my interviews with them in July 2003 in Cairo, broadly described
22   themselves as being less experienced and less responsible. In modern
23   times, mass schooling has played a crucial role in the production of
24   youth and prolongation of the time in which the individual lives and
25   operates as young. 'Youth' in the sense of 'behaving young' represents
26   a sort of Bourdieuian habitus—a series of mental and cognitive
27   dispositions, ways of being, feeling, and carrying oneself that are
28   associated with the sociological position of structural irresponsibility.
29   This is how young people experience 'youthfulness'.

30   Of course the reality of young people's lives is more complex and
31   may vary across cultural, class, and gender divides. For instance, many
32   adolescents in poor families may have to seek work to earn a living
33   instead of attending school; girls may get married early thus assuming
34   the responsibility of being a parent and spouse before experiencing
35   youthfulness; unmarried girls, even in the middle class families, often
36   take some responsibilities to help their mothers in cooking, cleaning,
37   or caring for the children. There is also the possibility of the young
38   couples who, once married, may appear as if they have moved out of

1   the youth world into adulthood (in 2016, 33% of Arab youth were
2   either married or divorced, and 15% of 'youth' in Egypt described
3   themselves as 'adults') (Friedrich Ebert Stiftung 2017). Interestingly,
4   anecdotal evidence suggests that the youngsters who did not
5   experience youthfulness in their young age may tend to 'experience' it
6   years after they move to adult life. A 40-year-old woman from Lebanon
7   stated recently that she did not want to get married and be responsible
8   at this age, because she 'had lost her youthfulness during the civil war',
9   and 'now want[ed] to experience it'. In fact, there seems to be a trend
10   of 30+ working or non-working women who do not wish to get
11   married but desire to live independently, while we also may encounter
12   young males who hold jobs and earn a living but remain unmarried and
13   live with parents.

14   How can we account for these sub-groups of the young? Are they
15   not youth? If they are, what make them so? Simply age? If so, what
16   then accounts for their positionality in the social structure? The
17   relevance of these questions boils down to the reason we strive to
18   conceptualize 'youth' in the first place. If the purpose is to identify
19   youth groups with particular needs and abilities in order to devise
20   policies to address them, then the particularities of such subgroups
21   should be acknowledged and highlighted. However, if the purpose is,
22   as in this essay, to understand what kind of politics youth espouse, then
23   we should focus on their positionality in the social structure to
24   determine if the individuals assume some sort of youth habitus or live
25   and behave like adults even in their young age.

26   **Youth Politics**

27   If we conceive of 'youth' in this fashion, youth politics then takes a
28   different form from what is commonly perceived and presented. In this
29   sense, youth politics is not the same as 'student politics', which is
30   concerned with student rights, tuition cost, and educational policies, as
31   well as contentions that are shaped by the school environment.
32   Curricula can potentially cultivate critical awareness about, say, racism
33   or colonialism, or a university's objectionable investments in certain
34   countries can potentially cause campaigns of divestment, all of which
35   are facilitated by the fact that college campuses bring students together
36   helping collective action. The protests in Spain's universities in 2010 or
37   those led by Camila Vellejo in Chile in 2011, concerning public
38   spending on education and an end to the commercialization of

1 schooling, exemplify what I mean by a 'student movement'. On the
2 other hand, youth politics is also distinct from such things as the 'youth
3 chapters' of different political movements or organizations, be they
4 Fascist, Ba'athist, or leftist. Rather, youth politics, strictly speaking, is
5 essentially about claiming or reclaiming youthfulness; it expresses the
6 collective challenge whose central goal consists of defending and
7 extending the youth habitus—a set of dispositions, ways of being,
8 feeling, and carrying oneself (e.g., a greater demand for autonomy,
9 individuality, mobility, and security of transition to the adult world) that
10 are shaped by the sociological fact of being young. Countering or
11 curtailing this habitus is likely to generate youth dissent (Bayat 2003).

12   Conceptual precision notwithstanding, real life is of course more
13 complex. The fact is that most youth are students, most students are
14 young, and almost all are at the same time citizens carrying broader
15 concerns. In other words, young people's politics encapsulate
16 contentions that derive from their multiple positionalities as youth,
17 students, and citizens, filtering through class, gender, racial, and other
18 identities. So even though young people often pursue their exclusively
19 youthful claims through cultural politics (e.g. in the way that the Iranian
20 youth followed particular a lifestyle in the 1990s), they may blend their
21 youthful claims with other concerns in their positions as students and
22 citizens to mobilize against corruption, political repression, or urban
23 exclusion, as we saw during the Arab uprisings and after. Yet in their
24 involvement in the broader political campaigns, the young often bring
25 to them a good degree of youthful tastes and sensibilities often
26 displayed in political graffiti, sociality, fun, and youthful energy.

27   The mere presence of young people subject to moral and political
28 discipline does not necessarily render them carriers of a youth
29 movement, because young persons (as age category) are unable to forge
30 a collective challenge to the moral and political authority without first
31 turning into *youth* as a social category, that is, turning into social actors.
32 Youth as a social category, as collective agents, are an essentially
33 modern, mostly urban, phenomenon. It is in modern cities that 'young
34 persons' turn into 'youth,' by experiencing and developing a particular
35 consciousness about themselves as being young. Schooling, prevalent
36 in urban areas, serves as a key factor in producing and prolonging the
37 period of youth, while it cultivates status, expectations, and, possibly,
38 critical awareness. Cities, as loci of diversity, creativity, and anonymity,

1   present opportunities for young people to explore alternative role
2   models and choices, and they offer venues to express individuality as
3   well as collective identity. Mass media, urban spaces, public parks,
4   shopping malls, cultural complexes, and local street corners provide
5   arenas for the formation and expression of collective identities.
6   Individuals may bond and construct identities through such deliberate
7   associations and networks as schools, street corners circles, peer
8   groups, and youth magazines. However, identities are formed mostly
9   through 'passive networks'—that is, instantaneous communications
10   among atomized individuals that are established by the tacit recognition
11   of their commonalities and that are mediated directly through the gaze
12   in public space, or indirectly through mass media (for an elaborate
13   exposition of 'passive networks', see Bayat 1997). As present agents in
14   the public space, the young recognize common traits by noticing
15   (seeing) shared symbols, for instance, inscribed in styles (T-shirts, blue
16   jeans, hairstyle), types of activities (attending particular sports, music
17   stores, and strolling in streets), and places (stadiums, hiking trails, street
18   corners).

19   Whether the young behave in their sheer youthful impulses or
20   respond to the broader and shifting power structures—of class, gender,
21   race, or age—has been widely debated, but youth political behavior
22   cannot conceivably be understood without considering the interplay of
23   youthful agency and societal structures, mediated by political culture
24   and political opportunity. Youthful claims are articulated mostly at the
25   cultural level and in the form of claims over lifestyle. But youth often
26   get involved in both cultural politics as well as wider political
27   contentions. Thus, to serve as transformative agents, the young would
28   often have to go beyond their exclusive youthful claims to draw on the
29   broader concerns of citizenry. Such was the conduct of the Arab youth
30   who played the leading role in the 2011 uprisings, opening a new
31   chapter in the history of the Middle East.

32   **References**
33   Abdalla, Nadine. 2016. "Youth Movements in the Egyptian Transformation:
34   Strategies and Repertoires of Political Participation." *Mediterranean Politics*
35   21, no. 1: 44-63.
36   Amara, Joumana. 2012. *The Youth Revolt: A New Frontier of Conflict.* United
37   States Institute of Peace: International Network for Economics and
38   Conflict.
39   Bayat, Asef. 2003. "Muslim Youth and the Claims of Youthfulness." In *Being*

1   *Young and Muslim: Cultural Politics in the Global South and North*, edited by
2   Linda Herrera and Asef Bayat. Oxford: Oxford University Press.
3   Bayat, Asef. *Street Politics: Poor Peoples Movements in Iran*. New York: Columbia
4   University Press.
5   Delgado, Magdalena. 2015. "Contentious Copts: the Emergence, Success, and
6   Decline of the Maspero Youth Movement in Egypt." In *Contentious Politics*
7   *in the Middle East*, edited by Fawaz A. Gerges. New York: Palgrave
8   Macmillan.
9   Desai, Raj, Olofsgard, Anders and Tarik Yousef. 2016. "Days of Rage and
10   Silence: Explaining Political Action by Arab Youth." In *Young Generation*
11   *Awakening: Economics, Society, and Policy on the Eve of the Arab Spring*, edited
12   by Edward Sayer and Tarik Yousef. Oxford: Oxford University Press.
13   Erlich, Haggai. 2015. Youth and Revolution in the Changing Middle East,
14   1908-1914. London: Lynn Rienner Publishers.
15

16   Friedrich Ebert Stiftung. 2017. Coping with Uncertainty: Young People in the
17   Middle   East   and   North   Africa.   Accessed   January,   24   2022.
18   https://mena.fes.de/fileadmin/user_upload/documents/FES_MENA-
19   Jugendstudie_EN_final.pdf
20   Kalman,   Samuel.   2003.   "Faisceau   Visions   of   Physical   and   Moral
21   Transformation and the Cult of Youth in Inter-war France." *European*
22   *History Quarterly* 33, no. 3: 343–366.
23   Keniston, Kenneth. 1972. *Youth and Dissent: The Rise of a New Opposition*. New
24   York: Harcourt Brace Jovanovich, Inc., p. 7.
25   Matza, David. 1961. "Subterranean Traditions of Youths." *The Annals of the*
26   *American Academy of Political and Social Sciences* 378, p. 110.
27   Nafaa, Hasan. 2010. "Egyptian Youth Knock the Doors of Change." *Al-Masry*
28   *Al-Youm*, January 3, 2010.
29   Passerini, Luisa. 1997. "Youth as a Metaphor for Social Change: Fascist Italy
30   and America in the 1950s." In *A History of Young People in the West, Volume*
31   *II: Stormy Evolution to Modern Times,* edited by Giovanni Levi and Jean-
32   Claude Schmitt. Cambridge: Harvard University Press.
33   Rowntree, John and Margaret Rowntree. 1968. "Youth as Class." *International*
34   *Socialist Journal* 25.
35   Salehi-Esfahani, Djavad. 2016. "Schooling and Learning in the MENA: The
36   Roles of the Family and the State." In *Young Generation Awakening:*
37   *Economics, Society, and Policy on the Eve of the Arab Spring*, edited by Edward
38   Sayer and Tarek Yousef, Oxford: Oxford University Press.
39   Sayer, Edward and Tarik Yousef, eds. 2016. Young Generation Awakening:
40   Economics, Society, and Policy on the Eve of the Arab Spring. Oxford:
41   Oxford University Press.
42   Shehata, Dina. 2012. "Youth Movements and the 25th January Revolution."

In *Arab Spring in Egypt: Revolution and Beyond*, edited by Bahgat Korany and Rabab El-Mahdi. Cairo: American University in Cairo Press.

Sukarieh, Mayssoun and Stuart Tannock. 2015. *Youth Rising?* London: Routledge, p. 81-82.

Touraine, Alain. 1968. "Des collectivités devenues explosives." *Le Monde*. March 7, 1968.

Turner, Ralph H. 1969. "The Theme of Contemporary Social Movements." *British Journal of Sociology* 20, no. 4: 390-405.

UNDP. 2016. Arab Human Development Report 2016: Youth and the Prospect for Human Development in a Changing Reality. New York: UNDP, p. 22.

www.ingramcontent.com/pod-product-compliance
Lightning Source LLC
Chambersburg PA
CBHW071749270326
41928CB00013B/2854